Kaleidoscope Facets
A Memoir of Darkness and Light

Kaleidoscope Facets
A Memoir of Darkness and Light

Frank Plasil

Cover Kaleidoscope drawing by Ivan Plasil

Kaleidoscope Facets
A Memoir of Darkness and Light
All Rights Reserved.
Copyright © 2021 Frank Plasil
v3.0

The opinions expressed in this manuscript are solely the opinions of the author and do not represent the opinions or thoughts of the publisher. The author has represented and warranted full ownership and/or legal right to publish all the materials in this book.

This book may not be reproduced, transmitted, or stored in whole or in part by any means, including graphic, electronic, or mechanical without the express written consent of the publisher except in the case of brief quotations embodied in critical articles and reviews.

Outskirts Press, Inc.
http://www.outskirtspress.com

ISBN: 978-1-9772-1906-0

Cover Photo © 2021 Frank Plasil. All rights reserved - used with permission.
Cover Photo © 2021 www.gettyimages.com. All rights reserved - used with permission.

Outskirts Press and the "OP" logo are trademarks belonging to Outskirts Press, Inc.

PRINTED IN THE UNITED STATES OF AMERICA

Dedication

To my Soulmate, Carol, treasuring her love, with gratitude for putting up with me through "thick and thin"

To my Great-Grandchildren, Godric and Archer, providing them with Kaleidoscope facets reaching back six generations

To my Granddaughter, Amira, courageous, kind, loving, and resilient

To my Son, David, honest, responsible, and always true to his principles

To the memory of my beloved Daughter, Maia, who lives forever in my heart and thoughts

To my Brothers, Ivan and George, with a salute to the bonds of brotherly love

To the memory of my parents, for their unwavering love and for setting me on the road to success, under difficult circumstances

Table of Contents

Foreword i
Preface v
Acknowledgements ix
Prologue: The Escape xi
Rise from Serfdom 3
A Family Divided 11
Surviving the Occupation 17
Tales from the "Liberation" 25
Beyond the Escape 31
New Roots 37
Pulling out the Roots 45
The New World 51
Catherine 57
A Kaleidoscope 67
From Sea to Shining Sea 79
Kaleidoscope Island Facets................................. 85
Secret City 93
Kaleidoscope Facets of Our New Community......... 99
Maia.. 109
Orsay 119
B. B. B. (Back to Berkeley and Back) 125
Around the World in 80-Plus Days –
   I Journey to Pakistan.. 133
Around the World in 80-Plus Days – II In Pakistan 145

Around the World in 80-Plus Days –
   III Journey from Pakistan 155
Carol 161
Return to Geneva, Switzerland
   and to Brookhaven, New York 169
The Tragedy of Maia 179
The Time has Come 185
Appendix I: Incident in Pakistan or, Fission:
   Nuclear and National 199
Appendix II: Brief History of
   Pakistan's Nuclear Bomb Program 211
Appendix III: A Note Regarding
   Scientific Publications 213

Foreword

Rarely do we experience an authentic story written with such razor-sharp precision, unparalleled clarity, and raw emotion as *Kaleidoscope Facets* by Dr. Frank Plasil. His collection of stirring vignettes draws readers in, transporting them to Europe, points in the U.S., the world of science, and the privacy of his personal life. Spanning a century, the story begins with his escape from Czechoslovakia and continues to the present.

The work of a significant figure in the world of science, *Kaleidoscope Facets* may surprise readers, particularly those who know Dr. Plasil well. The book differs greatly in style, tone, and form when compared to his impressive body of scientific research. The 500 plus published articles he has co-authored address weighty scientific topics of great consequence: the investigation of nucleus-nucleus collision at "ultrarelativistic" energies and quantitative studies in heavy-ion-induced fission. Of particular note is a theoretical paper co-authored with S. Cohen and W. J. Swiatecki entitled

"Equilibrium Configurations of Rotating Charged or Gravitating Liquid Masses with Surface Tension."[1] Considered a 'classic' paper, it has been referenced more than 1000 times."[2]

Dr. Plasil's impressive record of scholarly publications aligns with his career trajectory, which began during his doctoral studies in nuclear chemistry at University of California at Berkeley. His career path continued with research appointments at prestigious facilities in the United States, first at Brookhaven National Laboratory in New York and then the Oak Ridge National Laboratory in Tennessee. The latter encompassed his professional work from 1967 through retirement. In 1984, Dr. Plasil received the Alexander Von Humboldt Award in Germany. Adding to his distinguished record is the E. Mach Honorary Medal for Merit in Physical Sciences of the Academy of Sciences of the Czech Republic, which he earned in 1998.

In contrast to Dr. Plasil's scientific writing, *Kaleidoscope Facets* reflects literary quality. His words emanate a strong and passionate voice, inviting and evoking response. He offers vivid details in a methodical, uncompromising manner, balancing humor and tragedy. Capturing the peaks and valleys of life that all individuals experience, his personal story not only invites readers into his life; it will also stimulate their reflection on how to live. As written, Dr. Plasil's work bends from the

---

1   Published in the Annals of Physics, Vol. 82, No. 2, February 1974.
2   Our People. https://www.ornl.gov/our-people/frank-plasil. Retrieved December 8, 2018.

scientific realm, curving towards humanistic and artistic approaches. The images he presents and the metaphors he embeds create richly-layered narrative that will appeal to his readers' senses. Through the course of the story, he weaves together a number of themes in unexpected ways: family, identity, migration, assimilation, love, pain and loss, scientific endeavor, personal responsibility, independence, and redemption.

Readers will appreciate knowing how Dr. Plasil came to vision and compose this work. He is a recurring participant in a variety of courses offered by the Oak Ridge (TN) Institute for Continued Learning (ORICL). A Writing Memoir Program that I teach is among these, and he has participated in it for over three years at this point. Structured as writing group workshops, my classes rigorously follow a curriculum of writing theory and practice for the genre. During class meetings, participants discuss principles for writing, such as literary techniques, audience, voice, and other highly-specialized elements related to writing process and written products. Under my supervision, they also engage in practical exercises, such as presenting their work for discussion, reading it for response, and also serving as peer critics. In the end, the Program offers tremendous support for serious writers. For Dr. Plasil, this meant subjecting his work to intense review and revision. The end result: an exceptional literary work in its own right in the view of mature peer readers.

The integrity of Dr. Plasil's work is the outcome of our

interaction as two writers dedicated to a closely-held and valued story. What Dr. Plasil has acquired in the process reveals his willingness to absorb the insights I gleaned through my formal study of writing, my own writing and publications, my doctoral degree in the field, and my thirty-nine years' experience teaching writing, all genres, at the undergraduate and graduate levels. Within this context, he proceeded to write *Kaleidoscope Facets* to share the threshold events in his life in a memoir format. Readers will appreciate the authority of his work and the fresh voice of an author who does not hold back in the telling of his story.

Dr. Linda Best
Professor Emerita, English/Writing, Kean University NJ
Lenoir City TN
February 8, 2019

Preface

I was first inspired to write my personal story well before my life story extended to the teen years. The inspiration came to me as a child when my family was escaping our homeland, our destination not entirely clear at the time. Questions tugged at my mind as we continued our stealthy trek to the river. What about language, school, friends, and our futures, both as a family and as individuals, I thought. I knew the moment was pivotal. Life would never be the same. We would leave behind everything we knew, and I was certain that in time there would be much more to the story as we settled in a new country.

As time passed, the story I aimed to write expanded but also became more focused. I abandoned my goal of writing our full family story since we had dispersed. Instead, I concentrated on stories from my childhood and our escape up to the present moment. Lying within this framework are significant and meaningful narratives which I deliver through a unique form in this book—a series of vivid vignettes, short stories and scenes that delve into my deepest reflections on life, my disappointments and successes, personal achievements and personal tragedies. In one way or another, everything I share can be traced to that defining moment when we escaped, the circumstances that led to it, or the events that followed.

The vignettes I include in this book reflect the reality of my life and the decisions I made, for better or for worse. These scenes and stories are organized chronologically in the early chapters and then shift to a thematic arrangement for the reminder of the book. I cover a host of topics and concepts: family, identity, migration, assimilation, love, pain and loss, scientific endeavor, personal responsibility, independence, and redemption. Each vignette stands independent from the others. Themes and content rather than structure frame and unify this book.

Reflecting on the book's content, I've always felt its emotional weight—the full range of feelings, from the lowest point one can imagine to the pinnacles of life. As I developed the book's material, I detected colors in my work; these aligned different emotions with patterns of darkness and light. The peaks and valleys of my life stood out vividly, reminding me of a Kaleidoscope, and thus my idea for the book's title emerged.

My ideas for *Kaleidoscope Facets* foremost in my mind most of my life, the stories written in my memory rather than on paper, the how of getting my words onto paper into a published work was a stumbling block along the way. So accustomed to the scientific writing of my discipline, I needed support and guidance to shape my personal stories for a public audience.

While I was working, there was little I could do to follow my dream to write, but after I retired, my path became clear. Along with my lifelong motivation, I had the benefit of a local continued learning program, which offers rigorous professional courses on specialized topics. Among the many programs I pursued were two of great importance, general humanities courses and a writing memoir class. These served my needs for insights on literary writing and surpassed my expectations. For three years, I steadily attended a writing memoir class, which covered writing theory and practice for planning, developing, writing, receiving feedback, and moving on to publish personal stories. The peer response sessions in class during which I read my work and received feedback were both instructive and motivating. Within that context, *Kaleidoscope Facets* began to take shape and was completed.

Acknowledgements

I would not have been able to write and publish this book without the assistance of a large number of people: family members, friends, classmates, former colleagues and others.

My wife, Carol, deserves special mention because in addition to encouraging me and allowing me to get so absorbed in my writing that I neglected some household chores, she contributed in a major way to a number of the Vignettes.

I am grateful to my dear friend and colleague, Francoise Pougheon, for reading all first drafts of the Vignettes, and for providing crucial ideas and suggestions.

I appreciate the input of my brothers, Ivan and George, especially concerning family events described in the Memoir. Interestingly, in certain cases, their recollection of events is substantially different from mine, but that did not cause me to change my narrative. Ivan also provided the superb image of the kaleidoscope featured on the front cover of this book, and George located the meaningful old family photographs that enrich this work.

I am grateful to my Niece and fellow-writer, Tanja Plasil, who provided very critical but valuable insights.

Because I distributed drafts of the memoir freely to anyone who expressed a desire to read it, I was the beneficiary of many comments and suggestions, too numerous to list here.

I am grateful to Dr. Linda Best, Instructor of the ORICL Memoir Writing Program, and to its student participants. During the three years that I was involved with this endeavor, my work obtained the benefit of critical peer review and discussion.

Without question, the most important contributions to this work are those of my Mentor and Editor, Dr. Linda Best. These cover many areas, from encouragement; to providing numerous ideas both detailed and broad; to arranging the Vignettes into Sections; to editing, often several versions of the same Vignette several times; to help in deciding which images were appropriate and those that would show up well in black-and-white; to help identify a Publisher; to interacting with the Publisher and often interpreting communications that appeared confusing to me; to empathy and gentle "nudging" during my periods of "Writer's Block"; and to "pulling the whole project together." My gratitude is boundless…

Prologue
The Escape

Towards the end of World War II – the time of my earliest memories – I had gotten used to being yanked out of bed. But on this particular night, some four or five years later, when I was almost nine years old, the situation was different. There were no wailing sirens announcing yet another air raid. I was not taken hurriedly, in near-darkness, down the long zig-zag of concrete stairs, to a damp basement room, where we huddled by candlelight with other inhabitants of the apartment building. Then we had waited for the all-clear siren, listening to the "thud" of bombs and hoping that they would not find us. No, this time was different.

Being woken up in the middle of the night was the only similarity. Together with my brothers, aged four and five, I was dressed by our mother. This activity was also unusual, since the task typically fell to our governess. Father said quietly, almost gently, "It is time to go."

From the penthouse of the building, we took the elevator to the street and piled into the car, an "Adler," which was assigned to my father as a perk of his high-level government job. Little did I know that I was embarking on a journey of no return that would irrevocably change our lives forever.

The car was speeding through the deserted streets of Prague, the capital of Czechoslovakia and my birthplace. Soon we were in the countryside. With the moon behind them, the tall poplars which lined the road at closely-spaced, soldier-like intervals cast long shadows across our path. We raced through sleeping villages and towns. Father diverted my many questions by asking me to memorize the names of the towns through which we passed. "Someday, you may want to recall this journey," he said. This strange advice only added to the journey's mystery.

We arrived in Bratislava, the capital of Slovakia, where my father's sister and her family lived. My brothers and I were told to rest in a bedroom. My brothers gladly obeyed, while I pressed an ear against the door, catching fragments of a heated conversation.

"Leave your family behind. The Communists will not be able to hang on very long."

"You will be back in no time. Do not put them through it."

And, then

"I will not leave them behind. There is no way of knowing how long this will last. I would be lost without my family and would have no reason to continue. They might be condemned to a miserable life for decades."

Later in life I realized that had he left alone, we would have been separated for most of our lives.

When night returned, we were on the move again. After tearful goodbyes and embraces, we resumed our voyage by car. After only a short time, we stopped at the bank of a broad river, the Danube, as it turned out. Father told us that we were going on a great boy-scout-like adventure. He said we needed to be absolutely quiet. Not a whisper! If we remained silent, as a reward we would each be given a banana. I had no idea what a banana was, but it sounded exotic and would therefore be well-worth an hour or two of silence. Father saved some extra words for me: "You, as the eldest and as my namesake, you have the responsibility to keep your brothers quiet. Do not allow a single whimper to escape their mouths. Do not allow them to give the game away!"

We descended to the water's edge. Clouds covered the moon, and a light drizzle began to fall. I shivered despite the layers of clothes in which I was bundled. Now I believed that a few ghostly figures started to materialize from the darkness of the bank. Was this image a dream? Was I feverish? But no. A muffled sound here and there, the breaking of a branch, the shuffling of shoes through the leaves, all gave them away. They were real, and they stopped, crouching behind us. I was scared, but having been sworn to silence, I could not ask if we were in danger. Soon a small inflatable rubber boat arrived, together with a hooded, rain-coated "escape facilitator." Father and I were asked to sit on the floor of the boat. I could feel the water sloshing under the single rubber sheet on which we sat. We set out into the darkness.

After a while, we reached the opposite bank and disembarked. The boat vanished in the direction from which we had come and returned with mother and my two brothers. In vain, I wished so much that I could ask what was going on. We waited in silence on the bank, at the edge of a wooded area, which we could barely detect. Suddenly, in the distance, a light came on and dogs barked. My father stiffened and whispered a few words to mother. We then withdrew into the woods and continued to wait. Soon the boat returned with some of the ghostly figures from the other bank. Father approached them, whispered something to them, and they joined us in the woods. The boat disappeared again.

The boat came and went, until all ghostly figures were ferried across. Then, incredibly, several of the men among the ghostly figures, together with the oarsmen, began to carry the boat into the woods. We followed them in silence. The procession continued, stopping occasionally when we could see the distant light and when we could hear the dogs barking. Finally, we arrived at water's edge. How could that be? Did we not just cross the Danube? The only explanation was that we landed on an island, very probably in Czechoslovakian hands, and that we still had to cross the other arm of the river. And thus we repeated the back and forth ferrying of everybody to yet another, even more distant bank.

Dawn began to break, and the ghostly figures transformed into darkly-clad men and women. There were no children. A single car was waiting where we landed, and Father, after speaking to the driver, motioned for us to get into the back of the car. We took off, with the car bucking over the uneven gravel road that ran along the bank of the river. The hood of the car was adorned with two flags. I recognized one as being Russian, while the other flag consisted of two red horizontal stripes with a white stripe wedged between them. Only later did I learn that this was the flag of Austria and that we were travelling in an Austrian government car through the Russian-occupied zone of Austria.

Suddenly, Father shouted, telling us to get on the floor of the car so as not to be seen. The car slowed down at a check point and was waved through. This was repeated several times during the three-hour long trip, at the end of which we found ourselves in a large city – Vienna, the capital of Austria. Even though we were still in the Russian zone, Father must have felt greatly relieved, and we all breathed the air of freedom.

Epilogue

When the Communists took over the government of Czechoslovakia in March 1948 as a result of a coup, Father had to escape to avoid prison for being a prominent member of the Social-Democrat opposition party. Since the Social-Democrats were members of the ruling coalition of Austria at the time, the official car was arranged via Father's private Social-Democrat contacts.

From the Russian zone of Vienna, we made our way to the American zone having used forged passports, and from there we proceeded to the German-speaking part of Switzerland. We learned later that all the "ghostly figures" in whose company we escaped made it safely to freedom after walking at night across fields and woods through the Russian zone of Austria.

SECTION ONE

Rise from Serfdom

I remember my paternal great-grandfather clearly. When I was a toddler, he would shuffle about the huge mansion in Pilsen, the official residence of the Director General of the Pilsen breweries, his son and my grandfather. In a peculiar habit, my great-grandfather would often mutter to himself: "Ježiš-Marja-Josefe, Ježiš-Marja-Josefe, Ježiš-Marja-Josefe …," meaning Jesus, Mary, Joseph. I do not recollect my great-grandmother, his wife. But a wonderful photograph of an elderly couple has survived, my great-grandparents, holding a baby between them, myself. The lady's head is completely covered in black cloth, a sign of modesty, with her full face showing. The picture must have been taken around 1940, yet this style of dress is still the custom in several parts of the world.

Granted, my great-grandfather was not a serf. He was probably more akin to a sharecropper, although a few generations earlier, his ancestors were indeed serfs. Suffice it to say, he led the hard life of a subsistence

Grandfather František Plášil

farmer on a piece of land he did not own in Moravia (now Morava), a province of the Austro-Hungarian Empire. His genius, which resulted in our family's rise from rags to riches, was his realization that education was the key to everything. With tears in his eyes, my grandfather told me about the time when his mother cut off her hair and sold it so that he could go to school. We owe everything to these two humble and hard-working people, my great-grandfather and his wife.

Grandfather, no doubt realizing the sacrifices made so that he could prosper, was an excellent student, and after finishing his secondary education, he landed a job as a clerk in the brewery at Budweis, yes, of the original Budweiser fame. While there, he uncovered a plot of wrongdoing and embezzlement. He gained instant fame as a "whistleblower." In 1910, working in Budweis (České Budějovice), grandfather elevated his social status further by marrying one of the daughters, Anna, of a "bourgeois" family who owned a winery in town. Anna had four sisters and a brother, and her father was the mayor of Budweis. She became a valuable partner helping grandfather's spectacular rise in the business world with her common sense and social skills.

Grandfather and Grandmother Anna had three children. The eldest, František, is my father. My aunt, Božena, was born next and the youngest was another son, Zdeněk. Tragedy struck during the War, when Zdeněk, driving and carelessly overtaking, collided head on with a truck and was killed instantly. Being the youngest, Grandmother was especially partial to him and never fully recovered from the blow.

The Plášil family, Grandfather František, Children Zdeněk, František, Božena and Grandmother Anna

In his next career step, the "whistleblower" of Budweis was offered a position in the management department at the Pilsner Brewery. Despite its famous Pilsner name, grandfather found the brewery dilapidated and badly managed. He started a program of upgrades and enhancements involving both the plant itself and its reputation in the outside world. He had an interesting situation to work with. Unlike traditional businesses, with shareholders, boards of directors, etc., the ownership of the brewery was tied to physical houses that were designated as the "právo várečné," the "right to brew" beer. Thus, grandfather had to work with owners of the "right to brew" houses. As it turned out, he was very successful in this endeavor and got all the support he needed to turn the Pilsner Brewery into a world class enterprise, making it as famous as its name deserved. He became Director General of the brewery and moved into the newly-refurbished official residence.

There are many stories that date from the time between the two World Wars when my grandfather was the venerated boss of the world-famous Pilsner Brewery. The beer was called "Pilsner Urquell" in German and "Prazdroj" in Czech. He frequently travelled throughout Europe, visiting the many Pilsner franchises. He and Anna would be met at the railroad station by the local representative with flowers in hand. One story is set in Paris in the famous "Café de la Paix" next to the Opera. He relaxed there with the French representative and ordered a Pilsner Urquell. It was served in a very elegant fashion, together with a small tumbler of raspberry syrup. Perplexed, grandfather asked, "What is this for"? Slightly embarrassed, the local agent explained that the beer is always served this way because most Parisians found the beer too bitter and sweetened it with the syrup. Although not confirmed, it is believed that, outraged, grandfather fired the representative on the spot!

Grandfather was active in politics from his rise to power to the beginning of World War II. He was a mainstay of the conservative Agrarian party. He hosted

PLZEŇ. U Měštanského pivovaru. 91-?

The Pilsner Brewery at the time of Grandfather's "rule"

many influential people, including the prime-minister, Beran (ram, in Czech). Often, he would organize hunting parties on large estates that he either owned or on which he had the right to hunt game. In one such event, the hunting party formed a huge ring with game trapped in its center. The shooting started, and the ring would tighten. In an unfortunate shot, grandfather was wounded in his leg and had a slight limp the rest of his life as a result. It was said that Beran had shot him, but I am not sure that claim was ever verified. Grandfather led a grand personal lifestyle. He would periodically take "cures" at mineral baths, such as Marienbad, in the company of his mistress. He was a "ladies man." Anna knew about his dalliances, and she tolerated them for the most part. He liked to drive fast cars, bragging as to how many geese he managed to run over during a speeding trip from Pilsen to Prague. He was the cream of Czech society....

During World War II, Czechoslovakia was occupied by the Germans. Grandfather was allowed to keep his job as head of the brewery. He engaged in "passive resistance" by purposefully misdirecting shipments of German strategic value, etc. However, after the war, when the communists took over, he was accused of collaborating with the Germans, with the only evidence presented being the fact that he had kept his job. I am not sure what his punishment was in addition to his losing his job and having most of his assets confiscated. I think that he was banished from Pilsen and forced to live in modest circumstances in a village with relatives.

As was noted elsewhere, our family escaped from Czechoslovakia after the communists took over. At the time, we thought that we would never see grandfather again. But we did. As it turned out, my father worked for the United Nations in Geneva, Switzerland, and was tasked with writing reports on the economic situation in Czechoslovakia. The communists wanted these reports to be as favorable to them as possible and decided that, in order to achieve this, they would allow grandfather to meet us in Austria. A three-generation photograph of Františeks II, III, and IV survived. Later, to the bitter disappointment of father, I failed to produce František V, breaking the dynastic chain.

A Family Divided

Division within a family has occurred many times throughout history, has been heralded in Greek tragedies, told in accounts of royal intrigues, and romanticized in novels. A noteworthy example came about during the Civil War, when brothers fought brothers, and fathers their children, all driven by their individual beliefs in "the right cause." My family also had divided loyalties, but for very different reasons. Our tragedy was the result of the complex tapestry woven by the events leading to, and following, the First World War.

Before the Great War, my maternal grandfather, Ado, was a proud professional soldier. He was an officer in the army of the mighty and vast Austro-Hungarian Empire. The Empire, ruled by the notorious Hapsburg dynasty, subjugated many nationalities and ethnicities, including Croats, Serbs, Slovenes, Slovaks, Poles and Czechs. The hometown of my parents, Plzeň, or Pilsen as it was known then, was located in a part of the empire which later became Czechoslovakia. During a routine assignment before the war, Ado was stationed in Pilsen. There he met and fell in love with Maria, my grandmother. They had two children, a boy, Berta, and Eva, his two-year-younger sister, my mother. Although the parents spoke German with each other, the family language was Czech, as was its lifestyle.

Grandmother Marie Wengrová, Mother, and her brother Berta

During the Great War Ado did his professional duty. After the war, various nationalistic voices won out, the Empire was fragmented into many small nations, and Ado found himself, with some misgivings, a citizen of the recently created Czechoslovakia. Still, he was prepared to resume his career as a professional soldier in the newly formed Czechoslovak army. But this was not to be. Yes, the option was there, but he would have been second in every way, such as pay, pensions, advancement, etc., to younger men, who managed, one way or another, to change sides during the war and fight against the Empire. To Ado, what occurred was unacceptable on principle, and bitterly, he decided to leave the army and enter the civilian life of a Czech citizen.

Events in central Europe moved fast between the two World Wars, and Austria was essentially absorbed into the German Reich in March 1938 in an event known as "Anschluss." This was followed one year later in March 1939 by the German invasion of Czechoslovakia, when the British Prime Minister Chamberlain made it clear that the allies would not honor their treaty obligations and would not come to the defense of the Czechs. The consequences of these events on our family were traumatic for many reasons, but the immediate problem was the quick determination that Berta, by virtue of his Austrian father, was to be drafted into the German army. Several efforts were made to avoid this, including failed attempts to break his arm on the edge of a bathtub. In the end, Berta was forced to join the Wehrmacht, the

German Army, was dispatched to Stalingrad, and was never heard of again. Due to the strong bond between Berta and his sister, my mother, she took this loss very hard and kept hoping for a very long time that Berta was one of the very few who survived the Stalingrad massacre.

Mother in her teens with her brother Berta

After the Nazis took over the country and the Second World War unfolded, the family hunkered down and made every attempt to live out the occupation without getting into trouble. All rooted for the Allies and, when possible, engaged in passive resistance against the Germans. All, that is, except Ado. Unaware of, or refusing to believe Nazi atrocities, this gentle but proud and embittered man was openly pro-Nazi, even, on occasion, wearing a Swastika. In spite of this, many of the family members loved him and told him good-naturedly, "Ado, you are a nice guy. But for what you are doing they will surely hang you when it is over." Vindictive as the Czechs were once the war was over, Ado would probably not have been in serious trouble since he never engaged in any activity that was harmful to others. Sadly, but perhaps also fortunately, we will never know what might have happened. Proclaiming that he would rather live fewer years and grant himself the things he loved, than more years by depriving himself, he died of an angina pectoris attack during the early part of the war.

There were other instances of divided loyalties in my family either through happenstance or through ignorance. There was aunt Lea, Ado's older sister, living in Austria with a boyfriend from Berlin. She was nationalistic and in favor of the German annexation of Austria. She survived the war and lived for many more years. I knew her as a lively dear old lady who liked to sip wine and sing out of tune. In occasional serious conversations, she was sorry about her earlier views sympathetic to the Nazis, not having been aware of the full range of atrocities that were committed by them.

There was also my father's much younger cousin, Bruno, whose mother was Czech and whose father was an ethnic German from the Sudetenland part of Czechoslovakia. A few days before the end of the war, when it was already over in several parts of the country, Bruno showed up at our home wearing a German uniform. My father provided him with civilian clothes and helped him leave the country. After the war was over, the Czechs vindictively evicted all ethnic Germans from the Sudetenland, including Bruno's father, who later settled with my Czech aunt in Stuttgart. I visited them there once, and their bitterness poured out of them, accusing members of the family of not standing by them after the war. Bruno himself became a well-known professor with leftish leanings, teaching at a Swiss university.

Divided as our family was when it concerned the Nazis, this tendency was never the case when the next persecution befell us, this time by the Communists. All family members were always staunchly anti-communist, although not immune to accusations to the contrary....

Surviving the Occupation

On March 15, 1939, German troops marched into Czechoslovakia. They established the Protectorate of Bohemia and Moravia in the Czech region of Czechoslovakia and also established a separate protectorate in Slovakia. These events were rooted in the infamous Munich Agreement of 1938 engineered by the British Prime Minister Neville Chamberlain. In this masterpiece of appeasement, Chamberlain, Hitler, Mussolini and French Prime Minister Edouard Daladier agreed to allow Hitler to annex certain primarily German-speaking regions of Czechoslovakia (Sudetenland). This was agreed to without the acquiescence of Edvard Beneš, the President of Czechoslovakia, despite the fact that Czechoslovakia had a military treaty with France, which, in turn, had a treaty with Britain. Both France and Britain thus abrogated their treaty obligations in the Munich Agreement, virtually handing Czechoslovakia over to Germany and sealing its fate.

At first, there was little change in our family under Nazi

occupation. Father kept his job in Prague as the second in command at a large distillery, and grandfather continued as Director General of the Pilsner brewery. There were food shortages, but we were able to weather them thanks to our peasant relatives who occasionally, and illegally, supplied us with what the countryside had to offer. Another helping factor was the existence of a robust "Black Market," where everything had its price. There were amusing anecdotes concerning our food supply. When our country cousins planned to illegally slaughter a pig and wanted to let us know, in an attempt to outwit the German censors, they sent an open postcard with the message "We have slaughtered the agreed-upon item." They got away with it! On another occasion I am told that I loudly declared in a public tram, "Can we go to the black shop so that we don't have to croak?"

There was a tragic event that took place about midway in the occupation which, ironically, furthered my father's professional career. It started with the assassination on June 4, 1942, of the Nazi governor of the Protectorate of Bohemia and Moravia, Reinhardt Heydrich, "The Hangman" Heydrich was the Chief Lieutenant in Himmler's S.S. (Sturm Schutz, translation: Storm Protection) and was responsible for very repressive measures and mass executions. Hence, he became a prime target of the Czech underground fighters. He was gunned down in a bend in the road when on his way from his residence to his office. The site is commemorated by a large plaque. Enraged, the Nazis retaliated on the Czech population. They generated a list of the 1000-most prominent Czech citizens and earmarked them for execution. My father's name and that of his boss Ivo Pour were on the list. A cat-and-mouse game was next. The list of 1000 became known, and since my father's name was on it, he took off. It turns out that he spent days hopping from one train to another in an effort to elude detection while the executions proceeded. Fortunately, when somebody on the list could not be found, the authorities went to the next name. In this way my father survived while his boss and friend Ivo Pour lost his life and in turn Father ended up with Pour's job! Fueled no doubt by a guilty conscience, Father maintained contact and took care of Pour's daughter, Jitka Pourová, even much later when we were in exile. The retribution story did not end here. It also included the total destruction of a whole village, Lydice, with all inhabitants slaughtered.

Plášil and Pour families, Myself, Mother, Grandmother, Father, Jitka Pourová, Mrs. Pourová and Ivo Pour

The Jews in the Protectorate of Bohemia and Moravia were as much at risk as they were elsewhere in Nazi-occupied territories. For this reason the husband of my aunt Božena was smuggled out of the country and packed off to the United States. There he found somebody else, and my aunt ended up divorced after the end of the war. There was also mother's closest friend in Prague, who was Jewish. She was sent to the model concentration camp, Theresienstadt. My mother was able to visit her for a time, but one day she was no longer there and was not heard from since. She no doubt perished in some "liquidation" concentration camp. She had left her jewels with my mother, who gave a beautiful sapphire ring to my Jewish wife, Carol. A priceless memory.

As the war neared its end, we were subjected to aerial bombardments. These were announced by loud sirens. To this day I react inadvertently and strongly to any siren test. Most of the air raids occurred at night, and we would descend to a room in the basement, listening to the "thud" of the bombs and waiting for the "all clear." On one occasion when we returned to our penthouse apartment, we saw a huge fire a couple of blocks away. Apparently, a nearby factory sustained a direct hit. The bombardments were a far cry from the kind of surgical strikes that are possible today. It seemed as though the aircraft carrying the bombs were in a hurry to leave and dropped their lethal cargo randomly. For example, the National Theatre and the centuries-old Prague town hall were hit. The town hall burned for several days, and I remember being taken downtown to witness the spectacle. We had mixed feelings about the air raids. The planes bombing us were allied planes, and we rooted for them. On the other hand, nobody likes to have bombs fall on them.

The war took longer to end in Prague than anywhere else. The local Nazi contingent decided in early May 1945 that they had nothing to lose by extending the occupation of Prague. Realizing that the war had ended everywhere else in central Europe, the Czechs staged a three-day revolution. Father, with his pre-war military experience as a cavalry officer, commanded a squadron of captured Nazi tanks. And, thus, the Nazi occupation came to an end.

SECTION TWO

Tales from the "Liberation"

After the end of World War II, Czechoslovakia enjoyed almost three years (May 1945 to February 1948) of peace and democracy, until a 41-year dark curtain of absolute communist rule descended on the helpless country. Much had happened during those three years, including free elections. The formal end of the war in the Protectorate of Bohemia and Moravia was due to a series of "liberation" events. Earlier in 1944 at the Yalta Conference, Stalin and Roosevelt agreed to so-called "spheres of influence" in central Europe. These "spheres" bisected Czechoslovakia so that Plzeň (Pilsen) was in the U.S. "sphere" and Prague in the Russian "sphere."

Liberating U.S. troops arrived in Plzen on schedule, and the Americans were warmly welcomed by the population. There was much joyful fraternization and bartering for nylon stockings, chewing gum, and other unavailable items. A number of babies of mixed race were an unanticipated result. The Russian Red Army "liberation" troops were delayed because they were mopping up pockets of resistance in Berlin. Their Prague welcome was somewhat reserved, mostly due to their behavior. The anecdotes outlined below range from comical to sad. As the "liberating" troops arrived in the outskirts of Prague where we lived, a Russian soldier, apparently drunk, tumbled from the rear seat of a motorcycle, hit his head on the curb, and died. Witnessing this left a deep impression on me. How sad to survive a bloody war and triumph, only to die mindlessly in a drunken stupor.

The Russians had to have their vodka. Somehow a number of Russian officers came to know that my father was the head of a large distillery. One day, a couple of them arrived at our apartment asking Father for a bottle of vodka and offering him a horse for it. Father knew that if he were to give them a full bottle, they would drink it on the spot and require him to join them in many toasts. So, Father said that he had only a quarter of a bottle of vodka, and he gave it to them. After considerable time, two orderlies appeared at our door, lugging a huge item. It turned out to be the hind quarter of a horse. "For a full bottle of vodka, a horse. For a quarter bottle of vodka, a quarter of a horse." We were glad to have it. It provided us with scarce meat that lasted for some time.

Some of the Russian troops must have come from very "primitive" circumstances. For example, they thought that flushing toilets were meant for the washing of feet. They thought that modest little houses of Czech workers must belong to capitalists, since they included such luxuries as radios, running water, and indoor toilets. So, it was OK to rob these capitalists. Their idea of fishing was to throw a hand grenade into a pond or river and scoop up the carnage. The following amusing story could not be verified. A soldier stole a new-looking bicycle and, with some difficulty, learned how to ride it. Then he saw a delivery boy on a beat-up bicycle pedaling and not holding on to the handlebars. The Russian stopped him and gesticulated that he wanted to swap bicycles. In astonishment, the delivery boy agreed and whizzed away. The soldier now tried to ride the bicycle without holding on to the handlebars. The result was predictable. In frustration, the Russian took out his revolver, shot the bicycle, and walked away.

Some sad and shameful events took place. Vindictive Czechs killed some ethnic Sudetenland Germans and deported many others to Germany. The killings were not sanctioned by the state, but the deportations were! As noted earlier, Father's aunt was deported along with her ethnic German (but Czech) husband. The rationale for the deportation of all ethnic Germans was that Czechoslovakia did not want to give the Germans an excuse to ever dismember it again.

After the war, Czechoslovakia was initially governed by a National Front Coalition consisting of Communists, Social Democrats and the right-of-center Czechoslovak National Socialist Party. Promised elections were held in May 1946. The communists were victorious in the Czech portion of the country garnering 40.17% of the votes, while the anti-communist Democratic Party received 62% of the votes in Slovakia. Thus, countrywide, the communists held a plurality (38%), but not a majority. Hence Edvard Beneš continued as President of Czechoslovakia, while communist Klement Gottwald was named Prime Minister.

Edvard Beneš

During the next two years the communists maneuvered by various means and tricks to gain full control of the country. Finally, in February 1948, the Communist Party of Czechoslovakia, with Soviet backing, took over the government. This marked the onset of four decades of communist rule and the establishment of Czechoslovakia as a satellite of the Soviet Union.

A poignant event took place on March 10, 1948. It was the mysterious death of moderate Foreign Minister Jan Masaryk, the son of the first President of Czechoslovakia, Thomáš Masaryk. He was found on the pavement in front of the apartment building where he lived on the top floor. It was never determined whether he was pushed from his apartment or whether he committed suicide by jumping. I suspect the former, given the local centuries-old tradition of "defenestrations" and the mindset of the communists.

The consequence of the tumultuous events of February 1948 was that Father decided he had to leave Czechoslovakia. While a Socialist Democrat member of the Czech parliament, Father sometimes voted with the communists, but most often with the opposition party. The communists did not appreciate this "swing" voting, and given their vindictive nature, Father felt in danger. Our first escape attempt was made in the western part of Czechoslovakia. Two border guards were paid to lead us across the border. Unfortunately, their activities were discovered shortly before we arrived at their house and they themselves fled. Their house sported a sign indicating that it was confiscated.

Fortunately, nobody was posted at the house to catch potential fugitives like us. Our second escape attempt, this time successful, is described in "The Escape," elsewhere in this book.

Beyond the Escape

In early 1948, we ended up in the German-speaking part of Switzerland, and with the help of refugee organizations as well as Father's contacts, we were installed in a small apartment on the outskirts of Zurich, the largest city in the German part of Switzerland. The everyday language spoken there is Swiss-German, which is nearly incomprehensible to all other German-speaking people. Fortunately, Father had been exposed to Swiss-German, and to the Swiss culture in general, during his stay in Switzerland as a young man studying in St. Gallen for his Doctorate in economics.

Life was difficult for my parents during the first few months in exile. In spite of his Ph.D. and knowledge of German, Father was able to land only a poorly-paid menial clerical job. Mother had trouble understanding and speaking Swiss-German, had to prepare meals on a very lean budget, had no friends, and had no help with her three lively boys, including me. Part of the time during this phase of our life in Switzerland, I attended a very upscale private boarding school, the Institut auf dem Rosenberg, in St. Gallen. This was made possible by my father's connections, resulting from his earlier stay in the city. During my time at this exclusive school, I started to learn classic German, Hochdeutch, and was able to peep through a small window into the lives of the privileged Swiss.

In time, as Father got promoted, his salary increased and our situation improved. We moved to a quaint village, Erlenbach, situated on the shore of Zürchersee, the lake of Zürich. We lived in a spacious two-bedroom ground-floor apartment, from which my brothers and I could run out into the street and play with other children. We were enrolled in the local primary school, learning Swiss-German and Hochdeutsch, which was taught as a "second language."

Our family at Erlenbach, Switzerland

Father had several high-level Social-Democrat friends in the Swiss Government. One of them owned a vacation home in a small village in Ticino, the Italian portion of Switzerland located south of the Alps. I spent a summer vacation there together with the owner's son, Felix, who was close in age to me. We had a great time together, which meant we got into all kinds of trouble. On one occasion, when the lady of the house was out running errands, we decided that it would be fun to throw rocks onto the tin roof of a shed below our house on somebody else's property. The rocks made an ear-splitting noise and disappeared downhill by bouncing off the tin roof. Little did we know that the rocks landed in a yard full of chickens, killing and wounding some of them. Restitution had to be paid, and our leashes were tightened.

At some point during our stay in Erlenbach, I experienced a flashback to our Escape. Father reminded us of his promise that, if my brothers and I maintained perfect silence during the ordeal, he would give each of us a banana. Not knowing then what a banana is, we readily agreed. Over time, we forgot all about the promise, but, one day, Father showed up with the bananas and gave them to us. I ate my banana full of anticipation yet needed to hide my disappointment when I expressed my gratitude.

We could easily have settled in Erlenbach and led a quiet and happy life, except for two factors. First, we had only a temporary, time-limited asylum permit in Switzerland and were required to move on in due course. Second, Father's employment, while sufficient to sustain us, did not provide the kind of intellectual challenge that a person with a Ph.D. in economics is likely to aspire to. Hence, several efforts were made to find a country that would grant us permanent asylum. I clearly remember one of these efforts. We spent several days in a "camp" (yes, as in "concentration camp") sleeping in uncomfortable wooden bunk beds with thin mattresses, while being considered for immigration to Australia. In the end, after about two years in the German part of Switzerland, where I learned proper German that has stayed with me the rest of my life, we took off for England.

Life in England did not work out well for Father. He did not know English, in spite of intensive efforts to learn it, and we had very limited financial resources again provided by refugee relief organizations. We started out living in the center of London with all of us in one large room in the basement of a row house. For me, there were some interesting aspects to this arrangement. In the evenings, we had frequent Czech fellow-refugee visitors, who would argue with each other until late into the night about topics like the status of the communist regime in Czechoslovakia, the politics of Czech refugee organizations, the likelihood of return from exile, and so on. Engaged in clandestine listening, I lost a lot of sleep during those evenings, but also learned a lot about the plight of Czech refugees. There was also a huge benefit with our location in Stanhope Gardens, which were within easy walking distance to the museum district of

London. These museums were all free of charge, and I spent much of my free time there, especially in the science and natural history museums.

After a few weeks, we moved into a nice Victorian row house in Muswell Hill on the northern outskirts of London. The house was bought by an affluent Czech expatriate and was rented out for a nominal fee to Czech refugees like us. We shared the house with Blažej Vilím (formerly the General Secretary of the Czech Social-Democrat Party), his wife Mirka, and a few single refugees, one of whom painted a portrait of me that survives to this day. Except for the all-important fact that Father was unemployed, we resumed normal family life. My brothers and I were enrolled in local schools and participated in various activities such as going to the young people's movie show every Saturday morning. One serious problem that my brothers and I had to put up with was bullying and various other forms of discrimination. We were the "bloody foreigners." On one occasion the chief school bully suddenly put on a friendly face and offered me an apple. As I reached out to claim it, he cut my hand with a concealed knife. Often, my brothers were hit and pushed while walking home from school. I defended them with a hammer, the only weapon I could find. While staying at a boarding school in the summer, I got into trouble, because fellow students accused me of things I did not do. Even the teachers indulged in discrimination by always assigning me the worst chores, such as cleaning the toilets.

In the end, Father was rescued from his ordeal in England by a friend, Antoine Zelenka. Mr Zelenka worked for ILO, the International Labor Organization, operating under the auspices of the United Nations and headquartered in Geneva, which is in the French-speaking part of Switzerland. After the putsch in Czechoslovakia, the communists revoked Mr. Zelenka's citizenship. Stateless, he could no longer work for ILO. Father used his Austrian Social-Democrat contacts to obtain Austrian citizenship for him. In return, Mr. Zelenka found a clerical position for Father in the United Nations Economic Commission for Europe, and our family moved to Geneva, thus opening a new chapter in our lives. The Zelenkas had three children similar in age to my brothers and me, and the two families formed a life-long friendship both on the adult and youth levels. George Zelenka, one year younger than I, was my best friend until his untimely death from complications of a hernia operation.

New Roots

I regard Geneva to be my true hometown. I moved there in 1951 at the age of twelve. This is where I went to high school, where I spent my formative years, and where I was happy most of the time. It is also the place I returned to frequently during my professional career to work on the huge nuclear particle accelerators located there. Although Geneva is French-speaking, it is there, at the International School, that I became an English-speaking person. Simultaneously, I learned fluent French, mostly through daily interaction with the Swiss people. Two outstanding teachers at the International School led me to decide on a scientific career, cementing my future. Thus, the events in my life that took place in Geneva deeply influenced the rest of it.

Geneva is a place of great beauty. It is situated at the outflow of a large lake, Lac Leman. This lake is fed by water from high-Alpine melting glaciers, forming the headwaters of the Rhone, one of Europe's mightiest rivers. On clear days Mont Blanc, the majestic highest peak of Europe, reigns over Geneva's landscape. Except for a narrow strip of land which connects Geneva to the rest of Switzerland, the town and its associated countryside are surrounded by mountains that are all located in France. The city itself enhances the natural beauty of its setting. Located in the center of the old town on top of a steep hill, the cathedral dominates the city and reflects in the lake. Geneva has a rich history and an independent intellectual tradition forged by, among others, French protestant reformer John Calvin, French writer and philosopher Voltaire, and Genevese philosopher, writer and composer Jean-Jacques Rousseau. It is a place that is easy to fall in love with.

Our first home was a two-bedroom apartment on the first floor of a modest building. Father rode a bicycle to his job at the nearby European Headquarters of the United Nations (Palais des Nations). I commuted, first by bus and tram, then by bicycle, and finally by motorized bicycle, to the International School, located on the other end of town. My brothers walked to a local primary school. Mother stayed put, resuming her full-time role as exemplary homemaker. In a couple of years, as my father's career advanced, we moved to a three-bedroom apartment on the twelfth floor of a brand-new nearby building with plenty of room for all of us.

Our family life was close to ideal. Our favorite weekend activity was to find, together with some friends, an isolated place in the countryside, build an open fire, roast sausages, and share pot-luck dishes. On those occasions we played games, went for walks, sang, and enjoyed each other's company. In the summer we would go to a private beach on the lake reserved for employees of international organizations and their families. In the winter we made skiing excursions to nearby resorts in France, initially by train and later by car.

Plášil and Lydall family picnic

From spring to late autumn, my parents were active in the United Nations tennis club, and it was there that they met the Mucha family. Mr. Mucha was Polish, and Mme. Mucha was from Fribourg in the French part of Switzerland. They also had three boys, who were somewhat younger than the three of us, with their eldest, Yves, and my youngest brother, George, being similar in age. Yves and George formed a life-long friendship. Mother and Mrs. Mucha also formed a close relationship. Like my mother, Mme. Mucha was a homemaker, and each morning during the work week, she and Mother would spend a short time together, sipping coffee, smoking, and comparing notes.

Typical of life in Geneva in 1950, before weekend evenings were taken over by television, my parents had a very active social life, going to and hosting many parties. The participants were mostly Father's U.N. colleagues. These parties could get very lively, with parlor games, singing and so on. In one parlor game, in order to retrieve a forfeit, the participant was blindfolded and asked to crawl around, groping legs, in an attempt to guess whose they are. Father put on nylon stockings and made sure that his legs were groped first. When asked whose legs they were, the unfortunate man said, "my wife's." On another occasion, when pointed to, the person had to sing, without hesitation, a song in English. Mother was pointed to and, not knowing what the words meant, she sang a song that my brothers and I taught her: "Listen to the f***ing bird, listen to the f***ing bird." A stony embarrassed silence descended on the gathering, there was much explaining to do, and I was in trouble.

The International School of Geneva, Ecolint, had a profound impact on my life. It had two types of students:

those who lived-in and those who commuted. The boarding students were typically the offspring of royalty, aristocracy, and rich executives, who came from all over the world. The commuting students were, like me, the sons and daughters of international officials and diplomatic personnel. Daily interaction with fellow students with such varied backgrounds was an education in itself, and I formed many enduring friendships, some lasting to this day. I also fell hopelessly in love with an heiress who had a royal pedigree, Gerarda de Orleans-Borbon. Geri and I maintained our friendship well beyond the Ecolint days.

At the high school level, Ecolint offered four separate curricular paths: French-speaking students were prepared for either the Swiss Matura (Swiss high school diploma) or the French Baccalaureate (French diploma), while English-speaking students were coached for either the English General Certificate of Education (GCE) examinations or the American College Board exams. I followed the English curriculum and studied for GCE exams at both the "Ordinary" and the "Advanced" levels. Ordinary level exams, usually taken at age 16, test for a broad-range general education, while the advanced level exams, taken two years later, test for specialized knowledge. My Advanced Level topics were Chemistry, Physics and Mathematics. I also threw in German, because I knew the language and felt that advanced-level literature studies provided a good counterbalance to my hard-science focus.

After the completion of my studies at the International

School, my goal was to study Chemistry either in Oxford or Cambridge. Unfortunately, this was not possible. My GCE results were more than good enough for admission to either university. However, at that time, both institutions required knowledge of Latin, which I did not have. Ironically, the Latin requirement was dropped only one year later. Instead, I ended up enrolling in a three-year "Special Honours" course in Chemistry at Queen Mary College, part of the huge London University.

I left Geneva reluctantly and doing so was a major turning point in my life. During my studies in London, I was often homesick and lonely and returned home every trimester and summer break. Following the completion of my undergraduate degree, my ties to Geneva were finally permanently severed after I decided to continue my studies in the United States. Throughout my life I have been grateful for all the unforgettable life experiences and academic opportunities that Geneva gave me, providing me with a unique foundation for further study and for a career in science in the future.

SECTION THREE

Pulling out the Roots

Several events accounted for the end of our idyllic life in Geneva. I initiated the change by studying in England and, later, by leaving for the U.S. to continue my studies there. Father contributed next. He always tended to be restless when it came to his professional activities, and in 1960 he succumbed to his disposition once again by accepting a temporary United Nations assignment in what used to be the Belgian Congo. At the time, the colony was in the process of obtaining independence accompanied by civil war and infighting among the leading politicians. Father was posted in the breakaway province of Katanga, which was at the center of the civil war, and where the U.N. attempted to exert its authority by pacifying the area. As a leader in the U.N. effort there, Father placed himself in physical danger and had some interesting stories to tell on his return.

In the fall of 1957, I started my three-year B.Sc. (Special Honors) course in Chemistry at Queen Mary College of London University, now "Queen Mary University of London Campus." Of the many colleges of London University I selected QMC due to its outstanding Chemistry Department. "Honors" courses at London University are very competitive. Honors award categories are: First-, Upper Second-, Lower Second-, and Third Class. If a student does not earn any Honors, he or she may either try again or settle for a "pass" degree.

I entered this program along with thirty-one other students, yet only seventeen completed the course with Honors. Being highly motivated to do well, I spent nearly all my time studying, with breaks only on weekends. During the first year I lived in the house in Muswell Hill, which I described earlier. From there I commuted on a scooter to the east end of London, where QMC is located. Later, I was forced to change my living arrangements for reasons given below. I did well in the exams, and at the end of the first year, I was headed for First Class Honors.

In summer 1958, I returned to Geneva to enjoy my break from academics with family. While there, a catastrophic event took place, and I will continue to suffer the consequences of it for the rest of my life. My parents, their friends, my brothers and I were enjoying a picnic in the countryside near Geneva. After lunch, together with my brothers, I discovered that many truckloads of sand had been deposited nearby for some reason, next to a road and at the base of a small hill. We had great fun jumping from the top of this hill into the sand and found ourselves buried to the waist. I had just bought a cheap camera, and we photographed each other as we leaped through the air. Wanting my picture to be the most spectacular, I took a running start, flew high through the air, and landed beyond the sand on some rocks, crushing both ankles.

My memory of what followed is hazy. Extreme pain. A break-neck drive to a hospital in Geneva. Doctors talking to each other, wondering what to do. Overhearing an exchange, "How can we possibly put the right ankle back together?" Finally, morphine and oblivion. I spent the next few months in a wheelchair with my mother pushing it when needed. I could not return to London for the fall trimester, but was fortunate that Phillip Armitage, who is a life-long friend to this day, sent me his notes from the lectures. Slowly I mended, graduating first from wheelchair to crutches and then to a walking cane.

On my return to London in early 1959, it became clear that I was unable to live as before in Muswell Hill and commute to QMC. I found "digs" in the idyllic community of Woodford Green at the north-eastern edge of Greater London. There is a direct subway line from Mile End Road, where QMC is located, to Woodford Green, and thus my new living arrangement was well-suited to my handicap. A friendly Irish landlady provided a full English breakfast and dinner every day, and I was free to resume studies full time. I worked hard, but because I missed some exams during the trimester I was absent, I ended up with Upper Second- rather than First Class Honors. Only one student from our group scored

First Class Honors and, tragically, he broke his neck in a Rugby game scrimmage a few months later.

Following my graduation, I was offered a scholarship to continue studies for a Ph.D. in England. It was rare for a non-citizen of Great Britain to be offered such a scholarship, but I decided that I would continue my studies in the United States. At the time I joked by saying that I was tired of the English weather. I rejected an offer from Yale University claiming that the weather there was too similar to that of England and accepted a teaching assistantship from the Chemistry Department of the University of California at Berkeley instead. Moving to the U.S. was my major factor in our family's "pulling out the Geneva roots." Mother was upset by my decision to move so far away from her, but admitted later that she would have been disappointed had I chosen an easy road rather than a challenging one.

Father completed the "pulling out of the roots." Sometime after his assignment in the Congo, he applied for a transfer to the U.N. headquarters in New York. This move turned out to have been a major mistake because he could not adjust to life in the U.S. After a couple further assignments in Africa, he ended up at UNIDO, the U.N. agency for Industrial Development located in Vienna. This was his final job, in a city after his own heart.

My brothers also left Geneva, although George, the youngest one, at first stayed on an extra year to complete his high school studies. Ivan joined me in Berkeley and started studies in architecture. George joined us after he left Geneva to study geology. Later, after a number of jobs in different parts of the world, Ivan settled in the Bay Area and now lives in Marin County across the Golden Gate Bridge from San Francisco. George fell in love with the daughter of friends of our parents, Edith, who was with them when they visited us in Berkeley. He followed her back to Vienna and ended up staying there although not with her in the end. Thus, the three of us are scattered, with Ivan in California, George in Austria, and I in Tennessee.

The New World

In September 1960, I departed for a new life in the New World. Securing an immigration visa to the United States was easy for me, not as challenging and controversial as it is today. At the time, immigration visas were awarded according to a quota system, and quotas were assigned according to an applicant's country of birth. Since under communist rule Czechs were not allowed to leave Czechoslovakia, my quota was undersubscribed. I was also able to claim "refugee status," and thus the International Rescue Committee (IRC) paid for my airfare from Brussels to New York. Today the IRC continues to hold the highest priority in my budget allocated to charity, and over the years I have repaid my airfare many times over in the interest of others who seek opportunity as I did.

In New York an IRC representative met me, briefly showed me around, and then put me on a plane to Los Angeles. There, I spent a few days at the lavish home of an Ecolint friend of mine, Barbie, whose father was a high-level executive in the Lear-Jet company. I was confronted by many surprising impressions during my first days in the United States. The very first was a Horn & Hardart cafeteria in New York, where I was treated to my first meal in America. It consisted of food plates retrieved from little windows and paid for by coins inserted into slots. I had no idea that such places existed. The next surprise came during a refueling stop for our propeller plane from New York to Los Angeles. In the small airport of a place called Las Vegas, incomprehensibly, most passengers rushed from the plane to machines which were armed with long levers and equipped with coin slots. They put coins into the slots, pulled the lever, and watched little pictures spin in a window. It seemed to me like a pointless waste of money!

The house where I spent my first night in America was located on top of a hill in the exclusive Bel Air district, overlooking Beverly Hills and West Hollywood. It was a marvelous place, with an incredible view over the sprawl of greater Los Angeles, that had been featured in *Architectural Digest Magazine*. Barbie was away at college when I visited, but her parents were very kind to me and patiently answered my many questions. They had two very large and expensive-looking cars with huge fins attached to the sides of the trunks. I found both the fins and the need for two cars to be very strange. I was accustomed to European cars which emphasize utility, are modestly-sized to navigate the narrow roads in small villages and towns, and seldom have non-functional embellishments of any kind, let alone such ostentatious ones as those "decorating" the cars of my hosts. I also received my first American gift: an immersion heater so that I could make myself early morning tea, a practice to which I am now addicted. To this day, I brew a cup of tea bedside before I get up.

After a few days, I continued to my final destination: the International House (I-house) on the Berkeley Campus of the University of California. This was a difficult trip. Arriving at the San Francisco airport, I did not realize that Berkeley was quite a distance away on the other side of a big bay. It took three different buses, many questions, and a short taxi ride to get me and my life possessions to the I-house. But I quickly cheered up when I was greeted by a familiar face, a member of the "Ecolint mafia," who happened to be on front-desk duty.

Within days after my arrival in Berkeley, I started work as a Teaching Assistant in the Chemistry Department. I was in charge of two twenty-student sections of the Freshman Chemistry course, which had an enrollment of several hundred. Students were assigned to specific sections based on their scores in entrance exams. One of my sections consisted of students near the top of the Freshman Chemistry class, but the students in my other section were at the very bottom. I found the difference between the abilities, aptitudes, and knowledge of the students in my two sections to be nothing short of incredible. In my bottom section, the students were not able to set up a simple ratio, such as "if four atoms of oxygen are contained in one molecule of sulfuric acid, how many oxygen atoms are needed to synthesize a sulfuric acid solution consisting of 940 million molecules?" On the other hand, the top students often knew more about certain chemistry topics than I did. Never in any of my experiences in the many academic institutions in Europe that I am familiar with had I ever witnessed such lack of homogeneity in ability and talent within the student body.

Simultaneously with my teaching duties, I needed to get started on a research project that would lead to a Ph.D. thesis. Having expressed an interest in nuclear research for which Berkeley is famous, I was directed to the huge Lawrence Radiation Laboratory located on a hill above the main university campus. Due to the influence of the famous chemist Glenn T. Seaborg, all low-energy nuclear physics research in the Lab was carried out in the Chemistry Division. I was asked to talk to several staff members, and as a result, Dr. Stanley G. Thompson became my Graduate Advisor. Because he was not a member of the University Faculty, my official graduate study advisor was the Director of the Chemistry Division, Professor Isadore Perlman. By mutual agreement, it was decided that I would study the heavy-ion-induced fission of a number of relatively light elements ranging from Erbium to gold. The heavy ions, nuclei of oxygen or carbon atoms, were generated at the Radiation Laboratory's Heavy Ion Linear Accelerator, HILAC.

Stanley G. Thompson

At the time of my arrival in California, Glenn Seaborg was the Chancellor of the University of California at Berkeley. He was the discoverer of Plutonium, co-discoverer of nine other trans-uranium elements, and the 1951 co-recipient of the Nobel Prize in Chemistry. But it was his co-worker, my Advisor Stan Thompson, who did nearly all the actual work that lead to Seaborg's Nobel Prize. Some people even went as far as to say that Stan Thompson was the man who won the Nobel Prize for Glenn Seaborg. In any event, due to Glenn Seaborg's strong personality, I ended up changing my professional field from chemistry to physics.

Although primarily an experimentalist, I also worked in theoretical physics. This I started during my Ph.D. studies, motivated by W. J. Swiatecki (Wladek), an English-educated scientist of Polish origin. Wladek was hired by Stan Thompson to provide theoretical guidance for the studies done in Stan's research group. Wladek became my friend and mentor, and our early calculations in the "Rotating Liquid Drop Model" were included in my Ph.D. thesis. Our final paper published in 1974 together with S. Cohen and entitled "Equilibrium Configurations of Rotating Charged or Gravitating Liquid Masses with Surface Tension" became a "classic" and was cited by other researchers more than one thousand times.

Initially, my life in Berkeley left no time for anything other than teaching and research. However, my teaching duties came to an end after only one semester, when I was offered a Research Assistantship at the Radiation Laboratory. Conveniently, my R.A. duties did not extend beyond my own graduate studies. This arrangement left time to find more congenial living arrangements together with some new friends and also to pursue romantic interests. Thus, I settled into a stimulating, pleasant and well-balanced life.

Catherine

At this point I realized that I was now a fully functioning independent adult. I was no longer dependent on my parents' financial support as I had been during my undergraduate days. When making decisions, it was no longer necessary for me to consider how these might impact my parents. This realization brought about feelings of both liberation and responsibility. Nevertheless, family members continued to be in my thoughts as I charted my own course, and family loyalty has remained with me to this day. I continue to have close relationships with my two brothers, although with the three of us scattered to different corners of the world, these are strained by the tyranny of distance.

My first major independent move was to find a new living arrangement. After one semester at the University's International House, I moved into a private rented house in Berkeley, together with four British graduate students. I had a big room to myself in the finished basement. A door from it opened onto a garden which featured a heated swimming pool. The whole place was ideal for hosting parties, and we certainly took advantage of this. The house was located fairly close to the campus, and I commuted first by bicycle, then by motor scooter, and finally via an old inexpensive car. I bonded reasonably well with my British colleagues, although I was never fully accepted by them. It was very well to have studied in England, but it was not the same as actually being English! We all had responsibilities in running the communal house, such as cleaning, shopping and, occasionally, cooking for the whole group. On one memorable occasion our entomology graduate student colleague attempted to treat us to a chicken from his laboratory that had been fed on by hundreds of mosquitoes. There were no takers!

As my personal life was progressing, offering me opportunities to learn more about myself as an individual, my experiments for the Ph.D. thesis were proceeding reasonably well conceptually and intellectually. Unfortunately, though, I worked under strained circumstances due to the research environment that surrounded my work. As mentioned earlier, I was studying the fission of relatively light elements ranging from erbium to gold. Fission, the disintegration of the atomic nucleus into two smaller nuclei, is a process that is normally associated with much heavier elements, such as uranium and plutonium. However, nuclei of atoms of lighter elements can be induced to fission if they are subjected to a disruptive rotational force. This force can be provided via collisions of the nuclei under investigation with heavy ions, which are nuclei of atoms of, for example in my case, carbon or oxygen. These heavy ions were generated at the HILAC (Heavy Ion Linear ACcelerator). The director of HILAC at the time was Albert Ghiorso who, like my advisor Stan Thompson, was a member of Seaborg's research team. After some time, it became clear to me that there was no love lost between Ghiorso and Thompson, and that my presence at the HILAC was a "thorn in Ghiorso's side." This was the first, but by no means the last, time I was exposed to personal hostility between respected and well-recognized scientists. I resolved to avoid ever finding myself in a similar situation but, as I will describe later, I could not avoid it altogether.

As was the case with my living arrangements, the only option was to make the best of a difficult situation. Ghiorso considered the HILAC to be, essentially, his private property. The usual method of allocating accelerator time based on written proposals submitted to a program committee did not operate at the HILAC. Ghiorso assigned a large portion of available accelerator time to himself, and he and his aides conducted experiments based mostly on his intuition. However, one 24-hour period per week was assigned to a Norwegian scientist, Tørbjorn Sikkeland, for the purpose of conducting fission experiments. I was told that I needed to convince Tørbjorn to grant me machine time so that I could pursue my fission investigations. I was able to do this by describing my proposed research to him. He was fascinated by the possibility that an element as light as erbium could be made to undergo fission, and from then on, it was easy for me to obtain the required HILAC time. Tørbjorn even made much of his experimental apparatus available to me, including the reaction chamber into which I placed my targets and detectors whenever it was my turn to use the accelerator. From my interaction with Sikkeland, I learned that initial skepticism can be overcome by sound scientific arguments leading to cooperation and good will.

During this intensive research period, I shared a cramped office with three other of Stan Thompson's graduate students, Reinhardt Brandt, Eldon Haines, and Don Burnett. Eldon and Don helped me during the long experimental hours at the HILAC, and we became close friends, staying in touch and keeping track of each other's careers for a long time after our graduate student days. In the confined office space, my desk faced the only window, which looked onto a footpath leading to the cafeteria. People walking to lunch from other buildings would often wave at me, including a lively young lady named Catherine Goldenberg. Occasionally, Catherine and I talked at lunch, and she once told me a funny story about her initial employment at the Laboratory. She was hired as a secretary in the Chemistry Division but was fired due to "disrespect." Apparently, when a senior staff member failed to meet an important deadline, Catherine joked by pointing two fingers at him and saying: "Bang, bang!

You're dead." This was sufficient cause for the office manager to dismiss her. She was reassigned to scanning Bubble Chamber data with the fancy title of "Data Analyst." She sat for hours in a dark room looking for rare interesting events recorded together with thousands of routine events on film and projected onto a huge table. She was in no danger of being disrespectful in this job.

One evening I ran into Cathy when I was doing laundry at a local laundromat. I was folding a sheet when Cathy took it away from me and proceeded to show me "the right way" to do it. Later we laughed over this pretext, as though there were a "right" way of folding a sheet. After finishing the laundry, I accepted Cathy's offer to have tea at her modest rental apartment. It turned out that she was recently divorced, had moved away from her home in San Antonio, and was raising her four-year-old son, David, alone. She had earlier converted to Judaism partly because her ex-husband was a Jew of Galician ancestry. Her ex never showed any interest in David, did not provide either alimony or child support, and later, when I petitioned to adopt David, he readily gave up his parental rights. Cathy had a lively mind, keen curiosity, and we shared liberal political views. We started to see each other frequently and often talked until late into the night. Ultimately, we became lovers. Due to shyness, I missed several earlier opportunities, and my involvement with her was the first intimate experience in my life.

Catherine, Myself, and David

Catherine

Woddy and Ivan

George and Dana

After spending about one year sharing the house with the British colleagues, my brother Ivan arrived to study architecture, and he and I rented an apartment together. Later still, my other brother, George, joined us, and the three of us, together with Cathy, rented a marvelous large house with a splendid view, high up on Berkeley's famous Marin Street. My research was progressing well, my relationship with Cathy had become serious, and we decided to get married. When I informed my parents, they were devastated for many, mostly prejudicial reasons: Cathy was a divorcee – I should marry a fresh young thing, like a debutante; Cathy was three years older than I – this would surely cause problems as we grow older, and I should marry somebody significantly younger than myself, following in my parents' footsteps; Cathy was Jewish – yes, there was prejudice in the family on this score; Cathy was burdened by having a son, whom I would have to help raise without being equipped for such a task; Cathy had poor prospects for generating a lucrative income, nor did she have independent means; Cathy was not cultured and only had a high school education; Cathy was not sufficiently good-looking; etc. etc. There was one additional objection: "it is a bad idea to marry the first person one makes love to because curiosity will lead later to cheating in order to have other experiences. It is best to get this out of the system before marriage." Here, regrettably, my parents were right…

I had promised my parents not to get married before completing my Ph.D. work. Having finished my doctoral thesis and handed it in on December 31, 1963, in spite of my parent's continued bitter objections, and because we were in love, Catherine and I were married on February 15, 1964, at the Unitarian Church in nearby Kensington to the tune of Beethoven's 8th Symphony's "scherzando" second movement. The reception was held at the Marin house. Neither Cathy's parents nor mine attended the wedding. We left that evening for a honeymoon in Mazatlán and Guadalajara and spent our wedding night in a motel overlooking Monterey Bay.

Wedding of Catherine and Myself

A Kaleidoscope

"Look into the view finder of a kaleidoscope, and you will see images that look like constantly changing stained-glass windows. Kaleidoscopes blend physics with art in ways that amaze and delight."[3] No description could better capture my life in Berkeley, as a newly-wed, as the head of a small family, and as an independent researcher during that vibrant year from the spring of 1964 to the spring of 1965, when I left Berkeley for a position as a Research Associate at the Brookhaven National Laboratory on Long Island, N.Y. The Kaleidoscope images ranged from the peaceful beauty of camping and skiing trips, to the fascination of new research results, to a new and lasting friendship, to a painful examination of my relationship with David, and finally to the tumultuous birth of the infamous Free Speech Movement, at which I had a front-row seat.

---

3   "Facts about Kaleidoscopes," *Gift Basket*, Wednesday, August 21, 2013. Retrieved February 4, 2019.

The beauty of the many natural treasures of California cannot be adequately described, but memories of them arouse deep feelings even today. Our numerous camping and skiing trips, often together with my brothers, flood the Kaleidoscope with superb images. A campfire in Death Valley. The mirror surface of snow-rimmed Lake Tahoe. Tufa formations in Owens Valley's Mono Lake. The High Sierra campsite at "Let's Lake." The bubbling mud at Lassen Volcanic National Park, an intimate version of Yellowstone. The small lakes beyond Tuolumne Meadows in the high country of Yosemite National Park, recreated in Ivan's paintings. The tent on a cliff at San Clemente overlooking the Pacific Ocean, where we celebrated Thanksgiving. The quaint Carmel village and the breathless beauty of the Monterrey Peninsula. The magnificence of Hearst Castle at San Simeon. The deep blue, jewel-like Crater Lake. The enormity of the fog-shrouded redwoods near the coast and in the Sierra Mountains. The giddiness on the mountaintop at Squaw Valley when ready to take the plunge on skis. The dipping into ice-cold water at the "nude" pacific beaches. The soft sand of Stinson Beach below the towering Mt. Tamalpais, where I landed in a hang glider many years later. Such are the pictures that the Kaleidoscope has stored and often reveals to me in the shadows of silent thought.

But the Kaleidoscope is not limited to bright colors. Dark facets sometimes reveal themselves, as they did when mirroring my relationship with David, nine years old at the time. This was a serious problem for me, and I am not proud of how I handled things. There were occasions when I wanted to join my brothers, without notice, for some fun in the night. But we had no standing babysitter arrangements. Unfairly, I resented David for "grounding" me. I took out my resentment in a way that I now find as abhorrent. For example, David would get motion sick on some of our car trips and would have to vomit. Regrettably, I would call him "pukanski" at times like those. I only hope that my behavior did not scar him for life! Catherine was justifiably critical of my attitude, but we nevertheless decided to consolidate our family by having me adopt David. The process proved to be surprisingly easy since David's biological father readily gave up his parental rights, never having shown any interest in his son nor helping with his financial support. So, after he was tracked down, and after he signed the appropriate papers, David's birth certificate was changed to identify his father as Franz Plasil, a 17-year old student living in London, U.K. Our contact with David's biological father regarding the adoption process was the last we ever heard of him, and David and I have been father and son ever since.

The Kaleidoscope images now shifted, first from black to gray, and then still further to lighter colors. The legal issues were solved, but the emotional ones remained. I needed therapy to deal with those. During a session, I confessed that I did not "love" David as I thought I should, and a revelation followed when the therapist said that love was NOT a requirement. Kind and considerate treatment was a requisite, and I pledged to provide it. As it turned out, over time, consideration turned to empathy, and empathy, ultimately, to love. Of course, normal conflicts expected in any father-son relationship did flare up, and continue to do so, stoked by our very different personalities. But there is no point in dwelling on them.

Among the many highlights of the 1964-65 year was physics research that I participated in using the Radiation Laboratory's new 88-inch variable energy cyclotron. It was at this time that I met one of my most important professional colleagues and life-time friend, Harold C. (Chip) Britt. Chip was a staff member of the Los Alamos Scientific Laboratory in New Mexico on assignment in Stan Thompson's group. We performed a number of experiments together at the cyclotron, and we were co-authors of some of my earliest scientific publications. An expanded version of my thesis, with Chip as one of the co-authors, was submitted for publication in late 1965, as was a paper with just the two of us as co-authors entitled "Fission of Uranium 238 and Plutonium 240 Nuclei Excited by Inelastic Alpha-Particle Scattering." Our scientific collaboration continued over more than two decades, and our last paper as co-authors appeared in 1987. My Kaleidoscope is filled with many bright images mirroring our scientific collaboration.

Chip Britt

But the personal life of Chip and his wife Donna involves some of the darkest reflections that any Kaleidoscope can offer. In addition to Chip's professional activity, the Britts had a personal reason for spending time in the Bay Area. Unable to have children of their own, they wanted to adopt a baby. In a very bright Kaleidoscope image, while on assignment in Berkeley, Chip and Donna are seen to adopt a darling little girl, Beth. But tragedy struck several years later, when Beth was diagnosed with leukemia. She succumbed to the disease after a long and painful struggle. I know from my own experience that anyone who has lived through the loss of a child can imagine and fully grasp the wrenching agony that will haunt the parent forever. Such is the darkest possible Kaleidoscope facet. And tragedy continued to pursue Chip. One day in 1969, when attending a scientific meeting in Washington, D.C., and returning to his hotel in the evening, he was mindlessly stabbed in the chest in a robbery attempt. The incident resulted in a collapsed lung, and because of his limited breathing ability, in 1986, as he aged, he could no longer live in Los Alamos due to its relatively high altitude.

One of the most historically significant events of that colorful 1964-65 year was the "Free Speech Movement" born on the Berkeley campus of the University of California. I was fortunate enough to witness much of what happened first-hand. This was largely thanks to Catherine, who has always had a strongly-developed social conscience and whom I often accompanied to various demonstrations and political events. The Free Speech Movement got its start in the fall of 1964, when student activists, some of whom had worked to register African American voters in Mississippi in the Freedom Summer project, set up information tables on the Berkeley University campus and were soliciting donations for causes connected to the Civil Rights Movement. Existing rules at the time limited politically-motivated fundraising to Democratic and Republican clubs. On September 14, 1964, the University administration announced that existing regulations prohibiting political activities and fundraising by student organizations would be "strictly enforced." The first clash came on October 1st, when a former graduate student, Jack Weinberg, manned a Congress of Racial Equality table, refused to show his identification to the authorities, and was arrested. Hundreds of students surrounded the police car in which Weinberg was to be transported, resulting in a 32-hour standoff, until the charges were dropped.

On December 2, several thousand students gathered at Sproul Hall, the University administrative headquarters, requesting the removal of restrictions on political speech and action. The demonstration was orderly, and the students sang folksongs led by Joan Baez. Catherine and I were there when Mario Savio, a student at the time, passionately delivered his famous speech in which he pronounced:

> ... But we're a bunch of raw materials that don't mean to be......Don't mean to end up being bought by some clients of the University, be they the government, be they industry, be they organized labor, be they anyone! We're human beings! ... There's a time when the operation of the machine becomes so odious — makes you so sick at heart — that you can't take part. You can't even passively take part. And you've got to put your bodies upon the gears and upon the wheels, upon the levers, upon all the apparatus,

and you've got to make it stop. And you've got to indicate to the people who run it, to the people who own it, that unless you're free, the machine will be prevented from working at all.[4]

My Kaleidoscope reproduces this incredible spontaneous performance in all its brilliant and scintillating clarity, when I request it to do so.

But the event was not over. Together with the students, for a few hours, Catherine and I stared into a line of police motorcycles which confronted us, poised for action. At midnight, by which time we had left, a local deputy district attorney, Edwin Meese III, who some twenty years later became the 75th Attorney General of the United States, requested the Governor for authority to proceed with a mass arrest. About 800 students were arrested only to be released on their own recognizance after spending a few hours behind bars.

With time, the University officials backed down, and by January 3rd, 1965, provisional new rules for political activity on the Berkeley campus were announced. Sproul Hall steps were designated an open discussion area during certain hours of the day, and tables were permitted. Even though these rules applied to all political views, most identified the Free Speech Movement as a movement of the Left. In the spring of 1965, the

---

[4] Mario Savio, "put your bodies upon the gears" address delivered at Sproul Hall, University of California, Berkeley on December 2, 1964. American Rhetoric, https://americanrhetoric.com/speeches/mariosaviosproulhallsitin.htm, Retrieved February 6, 2019.

Free Speech Movement spawned the Vietnam Day Committee which provided a focus for the anti-Vietnam war movement.

At that point, we left the area for the next step in my career, a position as a Research Associate at the Brookhaven National Laboratory on Long Island, N.Y. When I first arrived in Berkeley in the fall of 1960, I found a placid conventional university. When I left four and a half years later, it was a hotbed of radicalism.

SECTION FOUR

From Sea to Shining Sea

In the spring of 1965, we loaded up our car with all our belongings and traveled coast-to-coast from Berkeley to Brookhaven National Laboratory on Long Island, N.Y., where I was offered a post-doctoral research position in the Chemistry Department. We made several stops along the way, many of them to see Cathy's family members. First, there was her elderly grandmother in Riverside, California. She was very sweet and offered to give us the first edition of a famous cookbook. Unfortunately, I persuaded Cathy that accepting such a gift appeared unreasonable. When her grandmother died a few months later, we could not find a way to acquire the priceless cookbook. We continued our trip via the Grand Canyon to San Antonio, Texas, where Cathy's parents lived. Cathy's mother had a civilian "hush-hush" job in the Air Force and seemed content. Her father was a teacher at a community college and a frustrated author. I was amazed by the number of interesting manuscripts he had accumulated and was flattered that he asked me to read some. In one particularly notable work, he described his life as a young, isolated watchman in a fire lookout tower somewhere in the Far West. He tried hard to get it published, with no luck. These days, he would simply publish his work independently.

We resumed our two-week-long trip along the "southern scenic route." Along the way, somewhere in South Carolina, we ran head-on into blatant racial discrimination. A chain breakfast eatery boasted in its sign at the entrance that colored people would not be served! For a moment, the statement knocked the breath out of me. It is one matter to read about overt racial discrimination in the news and in the material disseminated by the Civil Rights Movement, but the experience of being directly confronted by it is a completely different issue. I had the same reaction a couple of years later when, arriving in Oak Ridge, Tennessee, to take up employment at the Oak Ridge National Laboratory, I found that only one "enlightened" barbershop in the whole town was color-blind when it came to haircuts. Even though some clandestine discrimination remains to this day, I am happy that outward signs of it are rare.

During a snowstorm in late March, we reached our destination. The operation of Brookhaven National Laboratory was similar to that in other National Laboratories, but the culture among staff was very different. Probably due to the influence of the Ivy League universities of the North East which operated the National Laboratory at the time under contract with the Atomic Energy Commission, the research staff was structured according to an elitist tenure system, which was modified to serve the needs of such a large operation. Tenure-track staff members were recruited and provided with resources to perform innovative research. Post-doctoral research associates, like me, were part of the resources. The chosen junior staff members were also helped by a huge number of non-tenure-track staff who operated the accelerators and other research facilities. When the time came to either grant or deny the junior staff member tenure, the decision was based not only on the brilliance of the research performed by the candidate, but also by the need of the Department involved to maintain a sub-discipline staff balance. For example, a candidate who may have performed excellent research in nuclear chemistry may not have been granted tenure because the Chemistry Department needed to strengthen its Organic Chemistry branch. When I completed my post-doctoral appointment, I was offered a tenure-track position at Brookhaven. I was flattered and then asked the Chemistry Department Chairman, "Suppose that when I come up for tenure the Department is very happy with my research accomplishments, what would then be my chance of obtaining tenure"? His answer: "About 50%." On hearing this, I declined the tenure-track offer.

My research experience at Brookhaven was consistent with the "culture" of the organization. I was assigned to a junior staff member, Lou Remsberg, and we performed experiments together at the Cosmotron accelerator. The Chemistry Department had just completed a new building, and research associates like me were housed in alcoves which opened onto a long corridor that separated them from the offices of staff members. This was a change from when, even in the earliest days as a lowly graduate student, I shared an office with other students that had a door on it. In contrast, my workspace at Brookhaven created the feeling that "Big Brother is Watching You," under the guise of "stimulating open interactions." Remsberg and I published only two scientific papers together, with him as first author in both cases.

Regarding recognition of scientific contributions, the experience differed quite a bit from my Berkeley days. One of the requirements of our experiments was the simultaneous measurement of the time-of-flight and the energy of one of a pair of fission fragments. The fission fragment had to be free to impinge on a detector that would measure its energy, but it also had to trigger the time-of-flight apparatus without degrading its energy. I designed and built an ingenious device that accomplished this by bending and focusing knocked-out electrons from a very thin foil onto a time-of-flight start detector. Unfortunately, this achievement was never acknowledged anywhere! But in the end, I was very happy that I was instrumental in helping Lou obtain tenure, and we have remained friends for many years, often seeing each other when I returned to Brookhaven many years later to perform experiments on their new accelerators.

I worked at Brookhaven for about two years. One of the most important events of my life took place during that time, in November 1966, when I became a naturalized citizen of the United States. That occasion occurred a little more than six years after my arrival in this country in September 1960. The normal time between arrival on an immigration visa and naturalization is five years. My process took one year longer because, as was explained to me in one of the preliminary interviews, "We have to be extra careful with people working on atomic things."

During one of the interviews, I was asked to take the mandatory citizenship test in which the naturalization candidate is asked various questions regarding the Constitution and the Government of the United States. For one question, I was asked to name the Chief Justice of the Supreme Court. I had just returned from a job interview in Tennessee which then, as now, is a very conservative part of the country. During the trip, I noticed huge billboards proclaiming "Impeach Earl Warren." When on examination I was asked to name the Chief Justice of the Supreme Court, I was sorely tempted to answer innocently "Impeach Earl Warren," implying that "Impeach" was a fine first name for anybody!

The Naturalization Ceremony took place in a festive atmosphere at the Supreme Court of Suffolk County, Long Island, N.Y., on November 10, 1966. Sixty of us, almost all of white ethnicity, were naturalized in the ceremony, walking up to the Clerk of the Court to receive our Certificates of Naturalization. The Daughters of the American Revolution distributed small American flags to all of us, and we waved them dutifully, as we listened to inspiring speeches. I was proud to have become an American and still am to this day. Later, after Catherine's and my daughter Maia was born, I thought of the Daughters of the American Revolution. It turns out that Maia, through her maternal grandfather, could have qualified as a "Colonial Dame," thus, arguably, outranking a "Daughter of the American Revolution."

My personal life on Long Island, the topic for my next segment, was far more satisfactory than my professional life. The location allowed me to enjoy boats and the ocean to their fullest and instilled in me a life-long love for all forms of watersports, including water skiing and sailing.

Kaleidoscope Island Facets

During our years in Brookhaven, we rented two wonderful waterfront homes that were available at a reasonable cost only because the original owners, who either built or purchased the houses for summer use, now needed tenants to take care of their property year-round due to changed circumstances. Our first house was on the north shore of Long Island in Wading River on a high cliff overlooking the Sound. There was a sandy beach below the cliff, accessed by a long, gated staircase. Early on, I bought a leaky heavy wooden rowboat for twenty dollars and beached it below our rented home. I restored it, caulking all leaks and painting it. On weekends, we dragged the boat down the beach on rollers to the water and paddled around on the Sound.

Ivan serenading Grandmother Anna Plášilová

My love of water and of water sports can be traced to the days I spent on Long Island. Purchasing the rowboat offered me my first exciting taste of boat ownership, and many different types of boats followed, ranging from paddle boats, to kayaks, to small sail boats, to a competition ski boat, and even to a jet-ski. Unfortunately, the rowboat had a sad ending. When we moved from the Wading River house, we left the boat on the beach for occasional future use. The following winter, a huge storm destroyed the boat, and in the spring I found a fragment of it several miles down the beach, my unique paint job providing the means for identifying it.

Family gathering in Wading River, Long Island, New York

In our second year on Long Island, when the owners of the Wading River house sold it, we moved to a house directly on the water in Shirley. Located near one of the few bridges between the mainland of Long Island and Fire Island, its outer barrier, the house had a boat slip and was purportedly owned by a Mafia boss. Luckily, I had no contact with him since I dealt exclusively with a real-estate agent. The boat slip provided an irresistible temptation, and we bought a cheap, used out-board motorboat good enough for beginner water skiing.

Our boat in Shirley, Long Island, New York

The summer we spent in Shirley was one of the most wonderful periods of my life. We cruised through the waters sheltered by Fire Island all the way to Shinnecock Inlet, venturing into Peconic Bay and stopping to eat fresh seafood at the "Lobster Shack." We ventured into the open ocean where the waves were so high that our motorboat flew into the air, crashing down into wave troughs to the consternation of the Coast Guard, which issued us a "warning citation." We taught ourselves to waterski, observing peculiar results. Sometimes, in the duck-farm polluted bay, sea grass would wrap around the boat propeller, forming a "disc," and halting all forward propulsion. Slowly, we would sink into the murky bay, facing the chore of ripping the sea grass off the propeller.

During our first year on Long Island, there was a good deal of contact with my family because my father held a position in the headquarters of the United Nations and rented an apartment in a high-rise building in Riverdale, The Bronx, N.Y. Though Father was not happy with either his assignment or his living conditions, our proximity allowed for more interaction with him and Mother than we had in a very long time. We spent Christmas as well as many summer weekends together, and my brothers, Ivan and George, then living in Berkeley, joined us as often as they could. Although we had many good times together, the atmosphere was frequently strained. Unfortunately, Father had never accepted my marriage and would often openly insult Catherine, criticizing her looks and her management of the household. I was often caught in the middle and, in retrospect, I admit I did not properly support Catherine as I should have. Fortunately, my paternal grandmother, who was visiting my parents at the time, provided steadying influence.

Having rejected BNL's offer of a tenure-track appointment to the amazement of many, I spent a good deal of my time in the second year at Brookhaven searching for my next employment opportunity. I was fortunate to have several options, including offers from Oak Ridge, Argonne, and Lawrence Berkeley National Laboratories. Initially, I was very tempted to return to Berkeley. However, their offer was for a temporary position, which could become permanent later. Since budgets for basic nuclear research at that time took a plunge, I thought it safer to seek a permanent position. Perhaps I should have been more confident about my potential. In any case, I narrowed my choice to Oak Ridge and Argonne. In the end, my final choice of Oak Ridge was governed by two factors: the leader of the group to which I would be assigned and the probable quality of life at the two locations.

The Group Leader at Oak Ridge was Hal Schmitt. He had an excellent reputation and experience in the field of fission, which was dear to my heart. He was also developing innovative nuclear detectors as a private venture outside the Laboratory. The Group Leader in Argonne was John Huizenga, who was well known and worked on a broad range of nuclear physics problems. As it turned out, within a year of my acceptance of the job offer in Oak Ridge, Huizenga left Argonne for an appointment at the University of Rochester. As to the likely quality of life, differences between densely populated suburban Chicago and rural East Tennessee with its mountains and many lakes were obvious to me. It also helped that on a glorious day during my interview visit to Oak Ridge I was taken boating on one of the nearby lakes. I was sold!

My employment at Brookhaven ended in early June 1967, and I was not scheduled to begin work in Oak Ridge until mid-August. Consequently, we asked Catherine's parents to take care of David (11 years old at the time), and Cathy and I took an eight-week-long car trip around Europe, the first of my several "Trips of a Lifetime." We flew to London where we found the least expensive rental car with unlimited mileage. It was a tiny Mini-Austin, with four seats and a roof-rack for luggage. We drove through France to Geneva and then on to Italy, Yugoslavia and Greece. From Greece we proceeded to southern Italy via a car ferry and then returned to Geneva, where we met up with my brothers. They squeezed into the back seats of the "Mini," and we continued via the Swiss and Austrian Alps to Vienna for a grand reunion with our parents.

Ultimately, Catherine and I returned the car to the rental company in London, much the worse for wear. We then flew back to Tennessee. Catherine's parents put David on a plane, and we picked him up in Nashville, some three hours away by car from Oak Ridge. We needed to spend a night in Nashville and had trouble finding a hotel room. I wondered what was going on and learned the reason was the popularity of the "Grand Opera." I commented to Catherine, "We are in a place of great culture, where opera fills all hotel rooms." Of course, it was really "Grand Ole Opry"!

Secret City

I assumed my position at the Oak Ridge National Laboratory (ORNL) in August 1967 and remained an employee in the organization until my retirement at the end of 2002. I started as a regular Research Staff Member in the Physics Division, was promoted to Group Leader in 1978, to Section Head in 1986, and, finally, in 1999 to Corporate Fellow, the highest attainable level on the non-management career ladder.

I performed many experiments at ORNL, but also collaborated on research at other facilities, such as at the Super-HILAC in Berkeley; various accelerators at the European Organization for Nuclear Research (CERN), Geneva, Switzerland; and near the end of my career, the Relativistic Heavy Ion Collider at Brookhaven National Laboratory. Discussion about the actual research activities I undertook at both ORNL and additional facilities will follow in a later chapter. Curiously, the places where I worked on experiments outside ORNL, excepting the year I spent at Orsay, France, were locations where I had lived previously. These places were not the same when I returned at a later point, though. As Heraclitus wisely stated, "No man ever steps in the same river twice, for it is not the same river and he's not the same man."[5]

The existence of the Oak Ridge National Laboratory has its roots in the events of World War II, when the "Manhattan Project" was created for the purpose of developing the atomic bomb. In 1942, the Army Corps of Engineers established the town of Oak Ridge on isolated farmland near Knoxville, Tennessee, to house the facilities for this scientific endeavor. The considerations that led to the site's selection were relative remoteness and low population density, moderate winter temperatures allowing year-round construction, and the large amount of hydro-electric power available from the dam system of the Tennessee Valley Authority. At the height of war-time activity, the approximately 90,000 inhabitants of Oak Ridge were contained behind a network of security fences. All activities were classified as "Top Secret," and this marker earned Oak Ridge the nickname "The Secret City," a reference that has not lost its significance over time. Only very few individuals at the very top of the command and scientific ladders knew what took place in this Secret City.

The most important Manhattan Project site, and its intellectual headquarters, was Los Alamos Laboratory

---

5   Heraclitus of Ephesus. Wikiquotes. https://en.wikiquote.org/wiki/Heraclitus. Retrieved 20 July 2019.

in New Mexico. Robert Oppenheimer, often referred to as the "Father of the Atomic Bomb," directed the Laboratory; there the bombs were designed and the first test conceived. However, Clinton Engineer Works, the precursor of Oak Ridge National Laboratory, played an equally important role in the saga of the bomb, for it produced the material for the bomb dropped on Hiroshima. Identified as "Little Boy," this bomb was a simple gun-type device employing enriched uranium, as opposed to the much more complicated implosion bombs first tested in New Mexico and subsequently dropped on Nagasaki. Those bombs were called "Fat Man" and used plutonium produced in reactors at Hanford in the state of Washington, even though the ability of reactors to produce significant quantities of plutonium was first demonstrated at the Graphite Reactor located at Clinton Engineering Works.

Model of Little Boy, Atomic Bomb dropped on Hiroshima

"Little Boy" required uranium-235 that makes up only 0.7 percent of natural uranium, which consists mostly of uranium-238. Because the two forms of uranium are chemically identical and their masses are very close to each other, separating them proved to be very difficult.

Three methods were used in a process called "uranium enrichment," whereby the percentage of uranium-235 relative to uranium-238 is drastically increased. All three methods, electromagnetic, gaseous, and thermal, were employed at Clinton Engineer Works, but it was the electromagnetic approach, using huge devices called Calutrons, that yielded the highly-enriched uranium used in the bomb dropped on Hiroshima. "Little Boy" was such a relatively simple device that it was never tested before being deployed!

Model of Fat Man, Atomic Bomb dropped on Nagasaki

After the war, following a domestic debate over the permanent management of the nuclear program, the United States Atomic Energy Commission (AEC) was created by the Atomic Energy Act of 1946 to take over the functions and assets of the Manhattan Project. This transfer of oversight established civilian control over atomic development, separating the development, production and control of atomic weapons from the military. Military aspects were taken over by the Armed Forces Special Weapons Project (AFSWP). On December 31, 1946, the Manhattan Project ceased to exist, and at about the same time, the Oak Ridge National Laboratory came into being, featuring many basic and applied peacetime research efforts. In parallel, the population of the City of Oak Ridge decreased from the war-time high of 90,000 to about 30,000, which has remained constant to the present day.

Most scientists had conflicted feelings concerning the ethics and the need for releasing the atomic bombs on Hiroshima and Nagasaki. I have also had to face up to my personal feelings. I concluded that dropping the bomb on Hiroshima was justified in that it very probably saved millions of lives, since the fanatical Japanese would have likely continued the conventional war for a long time, until the bitter end. However, I believe that dropping the bomb on Nagasaki, which came only three days after Hiroshima, was premature and that the Japanese should have been given more time to digest the Hiroshima event. The one bomb might have been sufficient to end the war....

Kaleidoscope Facets of Our New Community

While still at Brookhaven National Laboratory, I attended a large scientific meeting in New York. There I met Bob Ferguson and Frances (Tony) Pleasonton, members of Hal Schmitt's research group at the Oak Ridge National Laboratory (ORNL), which I planned to join. The three of us connected immediately at the event and became life-long friends from that point. I have always been grateful for Bob's and Tony's friendship, especially the role they played in easing my transition from Brookhaven to Oak Ridge, both professionally and personally.

As mentioned earlier, we arrived in Oak Ridge in mid-August, 1967. We travelled by car from the New York area and experienced an immediate taste of East Tennessee as soon as we crossed the state line from Virginia. A huge roadside billboard greeted us with the words: "Seven Days without God Makes One Week."

It was located a short distance from that wonderful "Impeach Earl Warren" poster I had seen during my interview visit. Living in the state, following an assignment in New York, required an adjustment!

On arrival in Oak Ridge, we headed for the small "Capri" efficiency apartments, long since gone. Thanks to Tony, a pleasant note and breakfast food in the refrigerator welcomed us. Although Tony was a "Yankee," her gesture was Southern hospitality at its best! Tony soon introduced us to her friends Alvin and Marge Weinberg. Alvin, the Director of ORNL, became my close friend and mentor. Having one of the sharpest minds of anyone I have ever met, he asked me physics questions I could not answer up to one week before he died many decades later.

Alvin M. Weinberg

Our early personal activities in Oak Ridge included looking for permanent housing. We were fortunate to find a well-built house from the war era on Georgia Avenue, near the center of town, for a little more than $10,000. That house was not too far from those of Tony and the Weinbergs, who lived in appealing remodeled war-time homes. Our house consisted of a small kitchen, a living-dining room, and a powder room on the ground floor, and three bedrooms and a communal bathroom on the second floor. It also featured a large backyard which bordered on a greenbelt in the back. It was a modest yet more than adequate abode, the first of three in Oak Ridge.

Our first house in Oak Ridge, Tennessee

In contrast to our other friends, Bob Ferguson lived in

a beautiful and unique double-A-frame house, which he designed himself. He built it in 1964 in a newly developed area in the west end of Oak Ridge. His home had a view of the Cumberland Mountains in the winter, and, nestled in a grove of oak trees, it felt like a secluded treehouse in the summer. Instead of a front lawn, Bob planted some fifty hemlocks, effectively hiding the house from the street. I coveted the house from the first time I saw it and told him that if he ever wanted to sell it, he should bypass the market and simply allow me to buy it. Many years later, this transaction actually occurred, and the unique double-A-frame home became my third, and hopefully last, house in Oak Ridge.

We folded into the Oak Ridge social scene seamlessly, being welcomed everywhere. A favorite activity, especially for Catherine, involved the "Concerned Democrats" organization, whose major causes were opposition to the war in Viet Nam and to the "establishment" wing of the Democratic Party. Fundraisers, with drinks and country music, were held every weekend in the basement below a restaurant. We made many friends there with similar political views. In an effort to influence the Democratic Party from within, we joined it formally and became active to the extent possible. On one occasion, I was asked to pick up Senator Albert Gore, Sr. in some town on the Cumberland Plateau and bring him to Oak Ridge for a function. On the way, in Rockwood, we passed a factory spewing huge dark clouds into the air. Senator Gore proudly proclaimed that he was the one who brought the enterprise to Tennessee. This type of statement would not be politically correct today!

My professional life flourished at ORNL. I was engaged and productive. My accomplishments reflected not only my knowledge and motivation but also the support and collegiality of my work environment. I joined several research projects in Hal Schmitt's group, which had an active experimental program underway at the tandem Van de Graaf accelerator. In addition, with the help of various members of the group, I started my own research program at the Isochronous Cyclotron, leading the group in a new direction. In the period from 1968 to 1973, together with Hal Schmitt and various members of his group, I co-authored a total of nine papers published in open refereed scientific journals. I was the first author on two of these articles, which featured outcomes from my research program at the cyclotron. Of the other seven publications, six presented results obtained at the Van de Graaf accelerator.

Two additional papers I authored were published in the proceedings of conferences sponsored by the International Atomic Energy Agency (IAEA). The first, entitled "Neutron Emission in the Fission of Astatine-213," appeared in 1969, less than two years after my arrival in Oak Ridge. I presented it at the Conference on the Physics and Chemistry of Fission held in Vienna, Austria, in July 1969. On my way to that conference, I learned about the Apollo 11 moon landing and have never forgotten either event as a result.

The moon walk was a monumental feat for mankind, appealing to my scientific mind, the type that causes people to remember where they were, what they were doing, when it occurred.

Hal Schmitt

On the light side of my professional life at ORNL was an ongoing observation in my personal workspace. Our group was housed in consecutive offices in 4500-N, one of the Laboratory's main buildings. My office had a window on the face of the door and, in the interest of privacy, I attached a poster inside the door, facing out. An image of a beautiful naked woman entering ocean surf, the poster was very noticeable to all who passed along the busy corridor. I was amazed to find that many people would open the door and look at the other blank side of the poster in an attempt to admire the beauty from the front!

After some time, several changes took place at ORNL as well as in my career at the Laboratory. In the summer of 1971, the Electronuclear Division, which was the home for the Isochronous Cyclotron, was merged with the Physics Division, and its Director, R. S. (Bob) Livingston joined the Director's Division and established a small Planning Group. He persuaded me to join it, and I took a year off from research and accepted this staff position. The Planning Group reported directly to the Laboratory Director, and this experience, although "heady," convinced me that I was much happier doing hands-on research and that a staff position, no matter how important, was not something I aspired to.

After I returned to research, I shifted my attention to experiments at the Super-HILAC located in Berkeley, and for some time I did not lead any research performed in-house at the Laboratory, although I did participate in several experiments. Another change was the departure of Hal Schmitt, who left ORNL to pursue entrepreneurial interests in the private sector. During this phase of my career, in 1974, I accepted a one-year appointment as Visiting Senior Research Staff Member at the Institut de Physique Nucleaire in Orsay, France. I'll tell my story about that scientific and personal adventure later.

SECTION FIVE

Maia

When Catherine and I married, we committed to expanding our family. Unified in our hopes for more children, we maximized the likelihood of conceiving a baby, yet Cathy did not get pregnant. As a result, when I worked on Long Island, we visited the Margaret Sanger Clinic in lower Manhattan, now a U.S. National Historic Landmark, that served as a typical Planned Parenthood clinic in the 1960s, providing both family planning and fertility services. We utilized the latter, having artificial insemination with my sperm performed several times, again with no result. And then, when all hope was just about lost, our miracle occurred. On our return from a brief vacation trip to California in the summer of 1970, high in the Rocky Mountains, our daughter Maia was conceived. My joy was beyond description! I experienced the brightest facet of the Kaleidoscope.

I was elated by the prospect of finally having a child of our own, yet the pregnancy was unplanned and the timing unfortunate. I had committed to an assignment in Pakistan for a few months, and Catherine had always planned to accompany me on the trip. Of course, she could not do so while pregnant, yet I decided to go anyway, against the advice of friends. As it turned out, my absence was more than an annoyance. According to Catherine, she had a difficult pregnancy, and never forgave me for being out of the country in her time of need. On my return, our relationship deteriorated badly. Instead of rejoicing in anticipation of our child's birth, we quarreled and were both depressed. The kaleidoscope started to cloud.

On June 6, 1971, our Maia was born in Nashville, Tennessee. The reason for her relatively distant birth venue reflected our desire to both be present for our baby's birth. Nashville was our only option for meeting this commitment, for no hospital in the Knoxville area offered fathers that opportunity at the time. Thus, when Catherine started to have contractions, we set out on the three-hour drive from Oak Ridge to Nashville. Her water broke near Lebanon, about two thirds of the way to Vanderbilt Hospital. When we reached the hospital, we entered with urgency, rushing through the emergency room, and all turned out well. Our beautiful beloved daughter Maia was born in the early hours of that wonderful June morning. The Kaleidoscope shined brightly again!

Maia and Osita

Soon after Maia was born, we moved into a large contemporary house on Newcrest Lane, in the west portion of Oak Ridge, not too far from where Bob Ferguson lived. Our home had a kitchen-family room combination on the main floor as well as a living room, a room we converted into a formal dining room, a master bedroom with its own bathroom, a second bathroom, and a bedroom for Maia's use. The large finished basement consisted of a huge recreation room, a bathroom, and three other rooms, one of which served as my private space and office. There was also a small closet, which I converted into a sauna. I managed to own a house with a sauna ever since that time. The Newcrest house had an attached two-car garage and a large backyard, which I fenced in, so that Maia and a Great Pyrenees dog we acquired could roam around the property unimpeded. Cathy took up organic gardening, which was only modestly successful because she chose a section of the backyard that was not in full sun. But what she lacked in results, she made up in enthusiasm.

Maia

At about the same time, I made one of the best investments of my life. A friend of ours who was leaving Oak Ridge sold us a modest lakeshore property on Watts Bar Lake for $5,500. It had only fifty feet of lake shore and a small cinder-block cabin built by a modestly competent do-it-yourselfer. The property remains in our hands to this day and is the focal point for our summer leisure activities. Over the decades, it has undergone many changes. A few years after the purchase of the first cabin, I bought the adjacent one, which was also the result of an amateur effort. Later still, I had the two cabins torn down and replaced them with a beautiful, year-round, three-story house with open-beam construction, a spiral staircase, and a twenty by thirty foot "great room" with a fully equipped kitchen in one corner. It sits in the center of the two combined lots. Fixed and floating docks and a number of different boats complete this lake paradise less than half-an-hour from our Oak Ridge home, which means we can drive to it on the spur of the moment any time. Maia's earliest memories were surely of our lake cabin, where she learned to waterski at the age of three!

Lakehouse on Watts Bar Lake, Tennessee

Against this backdrop of prosperity and our delight over the birth of Maia, our marriage continued to deteriorate, our interests following different paths. Catherine concentrated on politics, her gardening, and advanced Transcendental Meditation. I took my solace in work-related travel and gave up on politics, since I was regarded as a "ferner" due to my accent, who should not be telling good Americans how to vote! In the summers, I enjoyed my time at the lake cabin, hosting an open house there every weekend, a tradition Catherine detested. Clearly depressed, Cathy no longer looked after herself. She gained weight and remained in her pajamas most days. We no longer enjoyed an intimate relationship, and I began to have interest in other women. Maia did not have a structured life, and Cathy would often lock herself up in the toilet for hours, reading romance novels. Despite the circumstances, I did not want our marriage to break up, because I could not stand to think about the possibility of losing Maia. At the time, Tennessee courts tended to award custody to the mother, no matter how undesirable the situation for a child might be.

Soon Maia showed signs of serious problems. She fantasized a lot, thinking that she was Wonder Woman. Many children will do this, but her therapist told us Maia actually believed this point about her identity! She continued therapy, but given the home situation, she did not improve, and the suggestion to institutionalize her came up in conversations about her well-being and care. Maia's health deeply concerned Catherine and me, and we sought marriage counseling as a result to learn if we could turn our relationship and home life around. To this end, we agreed to commit to therapy for two full years before reaching any decision about the future. At the end of the two years, in 1979, we decided to divorce. Catherine agreed to my custody of Maia, and a year or so after the divorce, she left the country.

When I became a single parent following the divorce, I experienced difficulty honoring my research obligation in Berkeley because finding adequate childcare was extremely challenging at the time. Despite social changes that increased the number of single-parent families and the number of women working outside the home, contemporary society had not yet responded to the need to care for children during work hours or professional travel. Fortunately, I found a person whom I regarded as an excellent caretaker for Maia during the times I had to be away. Maia called her "Nanny." She was a grandmother whose children were independent and who took other children in either overnight like Maia or just for the day. She provided a loving and caring environment, and I felt Maia was happy there. However, later in her life, when her anger with me was at its peak, Maia told me that she felt abandoned whenever I went out of town. If I had the chance to relive that period of time, I would definitely give up my Berkeley research in favor of taking care of my beloved and fragile Maia.

Our son David was fifteen years old when Maia was born. We watched him grow up with pride from a teenager to a young man of twenty-three responsible for his own future by the time his mother and I got divorced. He went through the Oak Ridge school system from middle school to high school and lived at home with us during that time. After graduation, he studied at the University of Tennessee, where he stayed in a dormitory and worked in the cafeteria to pay his way through college. He has been fully independent ever since.

Sometime in 1979, I fell in love with Carol Dittner, who was in the process of divorcing her husband. She moved in with me, and we were married in 1980. Soon after, we moved into Bob Ferguson's house, which he agreed to sell to me without putting it on the open market, as I had asked several years earlier. In many ways, life became easier, since Maia now had a stepmother to care for her whenever I was gone. Things were smooth between Maia and Carol when I was out of town. However, when I was home, due mostly to Maia's manipulation, an unfortunate triangle formed regarding shared relationships, time, and space, leaving the three of us angry, resentful, and unhappy with each other.

One time Maia ran away to a friend's house and later went to live with another "friend" in a dysfunctional family where she was abused in many ways. We actually paid for the privilege of Maia staying there! Although Maia could be sweet and even considerate at times, those instances were countered by periods when she was verbally abusive, telling me that she hated me and did not consider me to be her father. Finally, her psychologist, as well as the school authorities, deemed

Maia's condition pathological, and all agreed that in-house treatment was her only hope. The last straw came when her mother returned briefly from abroad to pick up a donated computer and sort out some of the possessions she had left behind. Maia, after interacting with her, had what amounted to a mental breakdown. As a result, in 1985, against her will, Maia spent six months in a local psychiatric hospital at the age of 14. This occurrence brought me more pain than I ever thought I could bear. I cannot continue the sad and tragic story of my beloved Maia at this time but will return to it later. That day, my heart was breaking, and the Kaleidoscope turned black.

Orsay

In 1974, when Maia was three years old, we spent a year in Orsay, France, located in the Greater Paris area. I had a very specific motivation for pursuing this assignment, which focused on the amount of disruptive rotational force any nucleus can withstand. As I mentioned earlier, under the guidance of my mentor at Berkeley, W. J. Swiatecki, I performed calculations in the "Rotating Liquid Drop Model" and included them in my Ph.D. thesis. The first paper I ever published addressed this problem. It showed that every nucleus has a limit beyond which it can no longer support the disruptive rotational force. A colleague, Marshall Blann, and I incorporated the Rotating Liquid Drop calculations into a model which predicted actual experimental limits on the observation of all nuclei.

Regarding these results, a research group in Orsay at the Southern Branch of the University of Paris challenged our predictions, claiming they observed nuclei that exceeded the rotational limit. I simply had to investigate their claim! To do so, I sought and obtained a one-year appointment under the title of "Visiting Senior Research Staff Member" in the group that published these results. It was directed by Marc Lefort, who along with the group as a whole, welcomed me with open arms. I proposed an experiment that would either confirm or refute the group's earlier results. It would utilize an electronic measurement method as opposed to the radiochemical technique employed to obtain the reported findings.

As soon as we gathered the required resources, we proceeded with the experiment. A number of Lefort's group members participated, including Lefort himself as well as two of the three authors, Gauvin and LeBeyec, of the paper that presented the questionable results. Together, we studied reactions of Ar-40 with a number of target nuclei at various bombarding energies, including the projectile-target-energy combinations of the original radiochemical work. Our results were submitted to the refereed journal *Physics Letters* on June 30, 1975, and were published on September 1, with the authors listed in alphabetical order. The paper asserted unambiguously: "Earlier results....appear to be in error...." (page 163)[6] It also stated, "The authors of [the work in error] believe... that part of the discrepancy may be due to... [a] case [where] cross sections for several products were obtained by interpolation (i.e., not via direct measurement)." (page165) Vindication was sweet! My year in France was scientifically productive over and above

---

6   Gauvin,H, and D. Guerreau, Y. LeBeyec, M. Lefort, F. Plasil and X. Tarrago, "Evaporation Residue Cross Sections from Reactions with Argon Ions. *Physics Letters:* 58B, No 2, September 1, 1975.

that particular outcome. Since I collaborated with the French group on several other experiments, I am the co-author of three additional papers published in refereed journals, including one in the prestigious *Physical Review Letters*.

Our year in France was also personally rewarding for everyone in my family. We traveled together on the continent while also pursing personal activities and interests. For me, perhaps the most absorbing activity was building a primitive hang glider and learning how to fly it. I did so near my rental house in Orsay, and with the help of a friend, I flew the glider from small hills in the surrounding areas. When the opportunity to join a hang-gliding school in the French Alps presented itself, I jumped at the chance. This program turned out to be an intermediate course for which significant prior experience, something I lacked, was necessary. The first flight required us to take off from a launch site and fly to a landing place that was not visible from the take-off area. With bravado, I took off and rounded the corner from which the landing area was supposed to be visible. I could not identify it, and so, to the amazement of motorists, I landed on a nearby freeway. On another occasion, I hit the gable of a three-story house near the designated landing area and gently slid down its side, tearing the hang glider in the process. Not surprisingly, I failed the course. Much later, in the San Francisco area, I purchased a professionally-made glider and learned to fly it properly. It was a joy to soar back and forth in the updraft along the cliffs of the Pacific Coast for as long as I cared to, being limited only by nature's call and the need to avoid collisions with other glider enthusiasts.

Hang glider

Catherine, Maia, and David enjoyed their own personal French adventures. Maia went to the equivalent of a kindergarten. She walked to school with her classmates and learned to babble in French as a result of her immersion in the language. The first French words she learned were "Laisse la!" This line translates as "leave her alone," something the schoolmates who protected her uttered repeatedly to those children who tugged at her or in other ways pestered her during the walk to and from school. Unfortunately, Maia later forgot the French she learned since she was too young to retain it.

Catherine was inspired by our year-long residency in France. She took the rapid train to the center of Paris several times each week to attend French lessons for foreigners, to take in the sights, and to visit the booksellers along the banks of the Seine. At home, she enjoyed all the fresh produce the local bi-weekly open-air market offered and worked on mastering the art of French cooking, to our great benefit. David, who was 18 by then, decided to visit Greece during our stay. While there, he met two French sisters who spoke reasonably good English. He took up with the older of the two, who initiated him in the "mysteries of life." He had a wonderful time!

As a family, we made good use of our time in Europe and travelled as much as possible. In the winter, we made several excursions to the mountains to ski. A notable trip occurred over the New Year, when we met my parents in Austria and celebrated the event with them. During the Easter season, the family enjoyed a wonderful road trip through Spain. The Kaleidoscope retains many brilliant facets from this trip, the highlight being the Easter Holy Week in Seville, with its remarkable processions, religious floats, and marching figures in their purple and violet robe-like, hooded costumes. But we also visited many other fabulous places in that marvelous country. The magnificent Alhambra in Granada silhouetted against the snow-covered Sierra Nevada; the mysterious mosque-cathedral of Cordova; the walled city of Avilla; the Alcazar of Segovia; the austere Escorial, seat of the Spanish kings and emperors; and the museums and culture of the country's lively capital, Madrid.

We had always enjoyed traveling, and our time abroad during my one-year appointment invigorated us, intensifying our interest in seeing the world. When our year in France came to its end, we were beyond sad and only reluctantly returned to Oak Ridge.

B. B. B. (Back to Berkeley and Back)

Earlier, I mentioned that following Hal Schmitt's departure from the Oak Ridge National Laboratory and after my year in France, my research interest shifted from internal ORNL investigations to experiments on the SuperHILAC in Berkeley. Several motivating factors led to this change. First, I regarded the research possibilities offered by the newly upgraded Berkeley HILAC, now referred to as SuperHILAC, as much more exciting than those available at ORNL. Second, I have always loved Berkeley and the Bay Area and looked forward to spending some time there. Third, an element of "escapism" also factored in, since, as described earlier, my marriage to Catherine was in trouble at the time; and finally, the two groups with which my ORNL group planned to collaborate were led by trusted friends, Chip Britt from Los Alamos Scientific Laboratory and Marshall Blann from the University of Rochester.

Our Los Alamos-Oak Ridge-University of Rochester collaboration had no official name, but it performed some of the most pioneering work at the SuperHILAC and was, consequently, welcomed as an outside user by the Lawrence Berkeley National Laboratory. During the ten years from 1973 to 1983, we studied heavy-ion-induced fission and mapped out parameters and limitations of other heavy-ion-induced reactions, including fusion limits and non-equilibrium particle-emission effects. We demonstrated that a correct quantitative description of heavy-ion-induced fission can only be obtained when nuclear finite-range contributions are included in the rotating-liquid-drop model description. Personally, relative to this research, I was rewarded with first-authorship on two scientific papers, including one in the prestigious *Physical Review Letters* entitled "Measurement of the Energy Division versus Mass in Highly Damped Reactions." Altogether, we published nine papers from 1973 to 1983, which was an impressive outcome.

We also provided a training ground for younger physicists. These included Hans Gutbrod, Glenn Young, and Soren Sorensen, who, at that time, published under his middle name, Soren Pontoppidan. I formed life-long professional relationships and personal friendships with these three individuals. Among many other roles, Hans Gutbrod became the leader of one of the groups of our WA80 collaboration at CERN, a story I will relate later. I was instrumental in bringing Soren to Tennessee and also played a role in Glenn Young joining my group at

ORNL. Ultimately, brilliant Soren became Chairman of the Department of Physics and Astronomy at the main campus of the University of Tennessee in Knoxville, and genius-level Glenn Young became the Director of the ORNL Physics Division for a period of time. I regard these two physicists' illustrious careers to be my most outstanding legacy, as I have always been happy to associate with individuals who outdo me in whatever skill or capacity.

Glenn Young, Soren Sorensen and Myself

My personal life during the periodic approximately ten-day-long trips to Berkeley was also very enjoyable and rewarding. Typically, I would stay, together with my colleagues, at some inexpensive motel such as the "Berkeley House" and commute to the Laboratory in a rental or government car. Often, I had to work during the midnight shift. On those occasions following my work night, I had the real pleasure of going, at 8 A.M., to a seafood restaurant near the motel, eating a crab omelet, washing it down with a Bloody Mary, and then tumbling into bed with the "do not disturb" sign on the doorknob, getting ready for the next "owl" shift. Since my marriage was disintegrating at the time, I formed one strong romantic relationship, which did not lead to anything close to permanent. In time, I realized that role was reserved for Carol, the lady I mentioned earlier.

The Kaleidoscope provides me with many other wonderful brilliant facets from the Berkeley trips. A bar called "Solomon Grundys," hanging over the water in the marina area of Berkeley, with the view of the fog rolling in from the Golden Gate Bridge during "Happy Hour"; an authentic Northern Chinese restaurant, "King Tsin," where an Israeli colleague of ours refused to use chop sticks, proclaiming that civilization has progressed from that primitive stage and then digging in with a hard-to-find fork; a noodle shop called "Ming Gay Ya" in a fashionable district near the San Francisco marina; and the home of the "Irish Coffee" near the wonderful "Fisherman's Wharf."

It is said, "All Good Things Must Come to an End." And so it was with our SuperHILAC work. Ironically, what changed our research focus was the construction of a facility that was underway in Oak Ridge: the Holifield Heavy Ion Research Facility (HHIRF). It was named after a U.S. Representative from California, Chester E. Holifield, who played a major role after the end of WW II in ensuring that all atomic matters passed to civilian control. HHIRF was an imaginative and daring project. It consisted of a folded tandem Van de Graaf accelerator enshrined in a huge tower, which graces the skyline of ORNL to this day. Radioactive beams from this accelerator were then injected into the existing 1963 isochronous cyclotron to produce the highest available energies of heavy ions.

Holifield Heavy Ion Research Facility, Oak Ridge National Laboratory, Oak Ridge, TN

HHIRF was a classic case of "Build it, and they will come!" When it was completed in 1983, we quickly turned our focus back to research in Oak Ridge and were not the only ones to do so. Scientists from other institutions with many great and promising research proposals also arrived to the historic "Secret City." They sought out our group, asking to collaborate with us. To the benefit of all, we provided local knowhow, manpower, as well as the required equipment, such as the reaction chamber and detectors. In addition, we had plenty of ideas of our own and were kept very busy and productive for years. From 1983 to 1990, we co-authored a total of sixteen papers published in refereed journals, many of them in *Physical Review Letters*, on topics covering a wide range of heavy-ion-induced reactions.

But even during this exciting research phase, we started to move towards much higher energies available at the CERN accelerator complex in Geneva, Switzerland, and as early as 1987 we had already reported preliminary results from our WA80 collaboration. I will cover this wonderful enterprise later.

SECTION SIX

Around the World in 80-Plus Days – I Journey to Pakistan

A number of similarities and differences link yet also distinguish my adventurous trip around the world from the stories told in Jules Verne's classic novel, *Around the World in 80 Days* published in 1873. Like Phileas Fogg, Verne's main character, I experienced unexpected adventures, found myself in great danger, witnessed events beyond imagination, and marveled at the range of sights and landscapes I encountered throughout the journey. The differences include the direction of travel: Phileas Fogg's was from west to east, whereas mine was in the opposite direction. Additionally, Phileas Fogg had a travelling companion, Jean Passepartout, while I was on my own. My trip was not motivated by a bet as his was, but rather by a two-month assignment in 1971 at the Pakistan Institute of Science and Technology, PINSTECH, under the auspices of the Agency for International Development. And, finally, I did not pick up a wife during the voyage; instead, my journey contributed to the breakup of my marriage to Catherine.

PINSTECH was founded in 1965 by the combined efforts of the Chairman of the Pakistan Atomic Energy Commission, Ishrat Usmani, and theoretical physicist Mohammad Abdus Salam, who was the Director of PINSTECH at the time of my residency there and who, later in 1979, won the Nobel Prize for Physics, together with Sheldon Glashow and Steven Weinberg, for his contribution to the electroweak unification theory. My assignment at PINSTECH was arranged as part of the Sister Laboratory agreement between the Pakistan Atomic Energy Commission and the Oak Ridge National Laboratory. A detailed account of this arrangement is included in "Incident in Pakistan or, Fission: Nuclear and National," an article I published in 1971 and have reprinted in this book (Appendix I). Part of the program involved the training of Pakistani scientists in reactor-oriented research at ORNL and then subsequently the sending of ORNL scientists to Pakistan to help them initiate their independent research. My travel to Pakistan followed the visit of G. Dastgir Alam, a Pakistani scientist in the Physics Division, whom we hosted for 15 months. Soon after he returned to his country in 1970, I left for Pakistan to help him get his personal research agenda underway.

My trip around the world began in January 1971. The first leg took me, along with Catherine and close friends Carol and Peter Dittner from Oak Ridge, to Hawaii. Catherine was due in late May yet already appeared as though she was seven-months pregnant. She complained most of the time, and the Dittners had to tolerate the situation and helped her after I left. I felt helpless but remained determined about proceeding with my trip around the world. Mercifully, after a few unremarkable days, we parted ways. I took a flight to Japan, and the rest of our group returned to Oak Ridge. In the years ahead, I returned to Hawaii several times, enjoying it under more favorable circumstances.

My kaleidoscope shows many fascinating scenes from my trip to Pakistan. On the way, I stopped in Tokyo, Hong Kong, Bangkok, Nepal, and several places in northern India. Often, friends of friends caught up with me and served as local tour guides. I learned a great deal about the places I visited, but sometimes found myself in embarrassing situations. The first incident occurred my first evening in Japan. A thoughtful colleague of mine treated me to the classic entertainment of a geisha lady. I was overcome with jetlag at that moment and exhausted. Before the entertainment even started, I was seated with my legs in a well that had a heater in it. I felt very warm and comfortable as result, so warm and comfortable that I promptly fell asleep as the geisha's performance began. What shame!! What a loss of face for the poor geisha. I have never forgotten this lapse in etiquette and have always hoped that she was able to live it down. What a waste of money for my kind and generous host.

But even before that loss of face and lapse of etiquette transpired, disaster occurred along the curb at the airport as I was being picked up by the elderly associate of my Geneva high school friend, Robin Penberthy. I'm not kidding when I tell you this associate's name was Shitoto, and when you learn about the debacle that played out at the airport, you will not have to think hard to guess the nickname I assigned to him! Robin instructed me to bring Mr. Shitoto the best bottle of single-malt whiskey I could find in the duty-free shop. I followed through with this request and was satisfied with the large bottle I purchased. As I attempted to board the car with the precious beverage in hand, the driver ripped it from me, and it promptly fell to the pavement, shattering into a thousand pieces. Had it not been for the glass, I would probably have attempted to lick the delectable fluid!

The rest of my time in Tokyo was only slightly less embarrassing. For some reason, the ORNL travel office arranged my accommodations in the very expensive five-star Imperial Hotel. In the evening I went out for a drink at a nearby bar, where I was served by an attractive lady who insisted on sitting next to me. I had no idea she was employed by a high-priced escort service, the cost of which would have absorbed all my spending money for the remainder of the trip. Fortunately, when I explained my ignorance, I was allowed to escape without paying anything beyond the normal charge for a drink. Although I did not tell my friends about that incident, they found it absurd for me to stay at the most expensive hotel in the country and moved me to a Spartan guest house, away from all possible cultural mishaps. My final kaleidoscope image from Tokyo is a serene scene at a temple, where many beautiful kimono-dressed ladies came with their gentlemen to deposit New-Year wish notes.

My next port of call was Hong Kong, where a different type of surprise awaited. Since I was on my own dime at this location, I arranged to be taken to an inexpensive rooming house in Kowloon, across the water from Hong Kong Island. Both the landlord and the taxi driver volunteered to procure a girl for me for the duration of my stay, on the assumption that I was one of the many G.I.s on leave from their service in Vietnam! A couple of days later, without a girl, I contacted the parents of Skip, another friend from my high school days. Skip's father was one of the Vice Presidents of Pepsi Cola, who at the time oversaw the East Asian market. For a few days I stayed at their wonderful house atop one of the hills of Hong Kong Island and recall a memorable excursion on their fabulous sailing yacht to the Chinese-junk-filled floating village of Aberdeen. Unfortunately, this adventure included an "Ugly American" comment by Skip's mother who, as our huge yacht pushed its way through the throng of small boats, gloated, "Look at all those little tourists stuck in a junk traffic jam!"

Departing Hong Kong, I flew over the bomb-crater, pock-marked South Vietnamese countryside, arriving in Bangkok, the capital of the Buddhist Thai Monarchy. At the time, Bangkok was a laid-back charming town. Unfortunately, during several subsequent visits, I watched it change to the hectic and congested city that it is today. The colleague of another high school friend took me to an old-style hotel, no longer in existence, across the way from the Grand Palace, Phra Borom Maha Ratcha Wang, which consists of a complex of buildings and was the residence of the Kings of Siam from 1782 to 1925. I spent a great deal of my time the next two days exploring the Grand Palace with its Temple of the Emerald Buddha, Wat Phra Si Rattana Satsadaram, regarded as the most sacred Buddhist temple in Thailand. The Emerald Buddha itself, Wat Phra Kaev, housed in the temple and pretty as a statuette, is actually a potent religio-political symbol and the protective image of Thailand. Another wonderful Bangkok sight is the symmetric "Temple of Dawn," Wat Arun, best viewed in the morning from a boat on the Chao Phraya River, the major river of Thailand. Overall, my brief stay in Thailand was one of much-needed serenity and rest.

My next stop, Katmandu in Nepal, was pure magic. Again, this description refers to my 1971 visit because the area has changed rapidly since then. I found an inexpensive room in the old town near the historic Durbar Square (meaning "Place of Palaces") and near the palace of Kumari Devi, the prepubescent "Living Goddess," worshiped by some of Nepal's Hindus. I got to see her as she waved coyly from her window. During my stay of several days, I tried to see as much of the Katmandu valley as possible, getting around on a rented bicycle for the most part, but also, occasionally, by rented car and driver. Rent-a-cars were not available, and driving them would have been too dangerous. When I had a car, I invited a young lady to join me. I met her as I was puffing on a hashish-filled pipe and we were both listening to improvised Hindu temple music. She was good company, and there was nothing romantic between us, despite the temptation. I visited the towns of Patan and Bhaktapur, as well as the holy places Pashupatinath, Changunarayan, Swayambuhunath and Boudhanath Stupa. When the time came, I reluctantly left Nepal, high in more ways than one and bound for Northern India.

A well-established tourist route across Northern India existed with airplane hops tailored to the purpose. From Katmandu the stops were Varanasi (Benares), Khajuraho, and Agra, ending in Delhi. The kaleidoscope has saved many powerful and beautiful facets from all these places. The first stop, Varanasi, is located on the banks of the holy river Ganges. At the time of my visit in January, the water level in the river was very low, and the palaces along its bank were just ornate mushroom tops sitting on high brown concrete pillars. I witnessed a fascinating event at night, when the body of someone who could afford it was cremated in an open fire by the extortionist "mafia" that had a choke-hold on this "holy" body disposal. More benign and picturesque was the early-morning shoreline activity. Ladies walked into the river with their saris on, washed themselves, and emerged clean and dripping. Men sat cross-legged, eyes closed, chanting mantras. Others brushed their teeth, washed their hair, or engaged in some other

Cremation on the banks of the Ganges, India

Morning activity on the Ganges, India

equally mundane activity. The shock came when, as I was ready to leave the scene, I saw the dead body of somebody who probably could not afford a cremation. It was floating by, with a bird sitting on it, pecking on its rear end. But at least the person did find his or her final resting place in the holy Ganges River! Witnessing this sight, the kaleidoscope suddenly sprang into action, recording the incredible image and engraving it indelibly on my brain.

Khajuraho was next. It is as different from Varanasi as possible. Nearly 100 Hindu and Jain sandstone temples, sitting on granite foundations, are scattered over many acres of a garden-like countryside with blossoms everywhere. The temples date from the Chandella Indo-Aryan period, 950 to 1050 CE, and are decorated with thousands of erotic carvings. These illustrate every possible coitus position, with couples sometimes aided by servants who hold the participants in the required position. Group orgies are also depicted in this catalogue of "classical porn." As beautiful and interesting as this UNESCO World Heritage Site is, like most visitors, I spent only the day there and continued to Agra in the evening.

Temple at Khajuraho, India

Agra is the "Mecca" of Indian tourism, and for good reason since it is the location of the fabled Taj Mahal. Although I have seen many pictures of this magnificent edifice, appreciating it in person that first time took my breath away. I have returned to the Taj Mahal several times, once to share it with Catherine and another time with Carol. I have a collection of photographs of this monument to love, taken from different angles, in different light, in different moods. But Agra has a lot more to offer. The massive Agra Fort, from which the deposed Moghul Ruler, Shah Jahan, imprisoned in July 1658 by his third son Aurangzeb, gazed at the distant Taj Mahal, the resting place of his beloved wife Mumtaz Mahal. Then there is Fatehpur Sikri, founded as the capital of the Moghul Empire in 1571 by the third Emperor, Akbar

(The Great), and functioning as the capital until 1585. Built from red sandstone, it encompasses both Muslim and Hindu architecture. Another lesser-known tomb is the jewel-like Itmad-ud-daulah, tomb of the grandfather of Mumtaz Mahal. After exploring Agra's treasures for a few days, I continued on to Delhi, arriving by happenstance in time to witness the incredible Republic Day activities.

January 26, 1971, Indian Republic Day was foggy and drizzly, yet these conditions did not dampen the prevailing patriotic spirit. I watched the long procession of armaments, flower-covered floats from various Indian ethnic groups, decorated elephants, and colorful cavalry. But the ultimate sight was that of Prime Minister Indira Gandhi, the daughter of Jawaharlal Nehru, the first Prime Minister of India. She was standing in a jeep, her sari gently flowing in a light breeze, waving to the adoring crowd. This extraordinary vision in view, the kaleidoscope could not contain itself. It sprang into action once again, registering the iconic figure with great tones and detail, ensuring it would forever occupy a front seat in my consciousness. With the parade over, I walked together with strolling multitudes around the beautifully illuminated Houses of Parliament. Thus ended one of the most memorable days of my life. Soon I continued on to my assignment in Pakistan, the story of which is the subject matter of my next segment as well as the article in Appendix I.

Around the World in 80-Plus Days – II In Pakistan

Soon after I arrived in Pakistan in support of the research of my friend and colleague, Dastgir Alam, I experienced my first glimpse of the magnificent Pakistan Institute of Science and Technology, PINSTECH. This Institute, which I describe in Appendix I, along with my scientific mission there, is located near the dusty village of Nilore, about twenty miles from Islamabad, the Capital of Pakistan. About an hour by bus from PINSTECH is the largest commercial city in the area, Rawalpindi, where I was housed in the palatial Intercontinental Hotel. During my spare time there, I roamed around old parts of the town on a rented bicycle, eating from food stands and drinking wonderful, cheap, fresh-pressed orange juice. I never got sick in the stomach except for one time, and that was after a meal served in my hotel. While exploring, I was always on the lookout for various artifacts, mostly brass and copper items, which I bought with pocket money

I was given in Pakistani Rupees. These could not be converted to western currencies, and I had more than enough for my local expenses. As a result of my ongoing search, I have a wonderful collection of various items, ranging from a brass samovar to a copper spice box as keepsakes of that momentous journey.

The highlights of my stay in Pakistan were a number of excursions, often with Dastgir Alam, who owned a car as a result of savings he collected from his hard-currency per-diems while on assignment in Oak Ridge. I was invited to Dastgir's house for dinner a few times, and I never got to see his wife on those occasions. She was in the kitchen and did not show herself. Dastgir would bring the many wonderful curry dishes to the small living room. We ate with our hands, picking up bites with Nan bread and keeping our fingers clean. It was only on our car excursions that I got to meet and interact with Dastgir's wife because there was no option for her isolation. In those circumstances, taking a photograph of her together with their young son was even acceptable. The customs I observed and learned about were all part of the de-facto social segregation of the sexes in a strict Muslim society. When I visited Dastgir's home village, the same custom applied, and except for an occasional very young girl, I never saw any females.

We had a wonderful time in Dastgir's village. The kaleidoscope shows a welcoming committee consisting of men, boys and three camels. Dastgir, another visitor, and I each mounted a camel and were led towards the central square accompanied in procession by the whole male population of the village. On the way, we passed a rickety wooden water wheel propelled by a blind-folded water buffalo harnessed to it and walking endlessly in a circle. This was the local irrigation method for whatever sparse crops the villagers were able to grow in the barren landscape. I, of course, was the center of great curiosity, openly stared at by all the boys and most of the men. Catching game birds with a trained falcon was another feature in our ceremonial welcome. In this case, Dastgir and I were spectators rather than participants. On leaving the relatively poor village, I wondered how it could ever have produced a nuclear physicist. In retrospect, I am surprised I never asked Dastgir that question.

Visit to Alam's village, Pakistan

Another memorable excursion occurred when I accompanied Dastgir to a wedding of one of his relatives. As was the case with nearly all marriages in Pakistan and India at the time, this one was arranged. The groom had never seen the bride before the wedding ritual, and during the ceremony, he only saw her face in a mirror as she sat coyly beside him. The male wedding guests never got to see the bride at all. One can only speculate what the wedding night was like. Surprise!! My collection of photographs includes several pictures from that beautiful wedding event. In one, the groom is seated between Dastgir and me. He is festooned with a huge tinsel-like colorful hanging ornament that covers his front side from his cap down to his knees. His face is further obscured by an upside-down heart that rests on it.

On another occasion, I took an exciting extended weekend trip to Gilgit, the northernmost territory administered by Pakistan. It is part of the larger Kashmir region, disputed by India, Pakistan and China. The area can only be reached from Rawalpindi by propeller plane with limited altitude capability. The flight skirts Nanga Parbat, which is the ninth highest mountain in the world at 26,660 ft. above sea level. It is the western anchor of the Himalayas and is so notoriously difficult to climb that it has the nickname "Killer Mountain." Due to the limited altitude that our plane was capable of attaining, it was unable to fly over the peak of Nanga Parbat and had to fly around the side of the mountain. It could do so only in good visibility, which we were fortunate to have on the day of our trip. We landed on a primitive runway in Gilgit, which was little more than a large dusty village set in a rocky and arid mountainous countryside. Soon the majestic backdrop of Nanga Parbat was shrouded in clouds, and this spelled possible trouble for us. We were scheduled to return later that day to Rawalpindi, but flying would not be possible as long as the big mountain remained invisible.

Nanga Parbat, District of Gilgit-Baltistan, Pakistan

Gilgit hospitality turned out to be wonderful. A local businessman invited the all-male crew of the aircraft and of the local airline office to a picnic in a side valley. We totaled twenty-four men and are immortalized in a photograph taken that day. The scene for our repast outdoors was exotic. Oriental carpets were spread on the ground, and large cauldrons of excellent mutton curry appeared as if by magic. We sat cross-legged on the carpets enjoying the feast. The pilot was revered as a demi-god, and I was the usual curiosity. As it turned out, we were stuck in Gilgit for a couple of days before the weather cleared long enough for us to take off for the return journey. I was put up in a Spartan guest house where I slept in my clothes and avoided drinking the local water. High-class entertainment was provided on one of the days in the form of a rambunctious polo game. I did not see a single female, old or young, during my stay in Gilgit. Once we were in the air on the return journey, clouds again concealed Nanga Parbat, but, fortunately, the pilot decided to soldier on, and we did not turn back.

I made one other excursion into the foothills of the Himalayas during my stay in Pakistan. It was in a four-wheel drive vehicle belonging to an English couple on some assignment in the Islamabad area. We decided to drive up one of the valleys on a barely passable road as far as we could go. We encountered terraced fields, first covered with winter wheat, then with dirt ready for planting, and, finally, with snow. I had to remind myself that the temperature in Rawalpindi was probably about 95 degrees at that time! The valley narrowed down, and there was little sign of life until we arrived at a small village complete with a primitive guest house and one all-purpose building serving as a store, a tearoom, and an eating place. Men with beards died orange were hanging around watching others pounding out Nan dough for baking. We enjoyed sharing briefly our life with them, communicating as best as we could. After spending a night on plank beds, and after paying with a few Rupees, we embarked on our return journey. On the way I actually saw, for the first time in Pakistan, the uncovered face of a woman in plain sight, on the open road. She was colorfully dressed, carried a large jug on her head, and stared at us with impunity. She was a "gypsy," and as such, she was not constrained by the strict Muslim rules. The nearby camp of her family consisted of a large improvised canvas tent with three camels tethered in front of it.

Another exciting excursion was to Lahore, the capital of Punjab province and Pakistan's second-largest and wealthiest city. The trip was carefully timed to coincide with Eid al-Fitr, the Festival of the Breaking of the Fast, which marks the end of Ramadan, the Islamic holy month of fasting. I witnessed the traditional ceremony in which thousands of men crowded into the huge courtyard of the Moghul-era Badshahi Mosque, praying in the direction of Mecca. While the men prostrated in prayer, their faces flush with the surface, a group of young girls in festive dresses scattered through the area, their heads rising above their prone fathers. Capturing the juxtaposition of solemn prayer and joyful youth, the scene was an amazing sight to behold. Lahore is a great cultural and commercial center with many beautiful buildings and monuments from past eras. It has a larger number of Moghul edifices than either Agra or Delhi. Lahore has changed hands many times from Moghuls to Afghans, then to Sikhs, and finally to the British. I enjoyed walking in the old city and the kaleidoscope stored many brilliant scenes. A herd of water buffalos trying to squeeze through a narrow medieval gate, competing with pedestrians, bicycles and carts; decorated sheep in a square waiting to be sold for the breaking of the fast; a dazzling array of sweets of all colors in the bazaar; and burka-clad ladies, their bodies totally covered from head to the ground, with only a mesh screen allowing them to see where they were going.

Eid, Grand Mosque, Lahore, Pakistan

My last trip before leaving the country was to the legendary Khyber Pass, the traditional invasion route from Afghanistan to India. I accomplished the trip in a taxi rented in Peshawar, a town near the Afghan border, where I stayed with Dastgir's relatives before setting out. They had a nice house on the outskirts of the town, and I remember an unfortunate bathroom incident from the time I stayed there. The toilet was of the standard type where one squats over a hole in the ground to do one's business. There is never any toilet paper, but a container of water is provided. The custom is to use the left hand to clean oneself, and then wash it with the water. Since I was never able to adopt this method, I always carried toilet paper with me. I made use of it, and as we were leaving the house, I noticed to my embarrassment that it had made its way to an open sewer on the side of the house.

The trip to the Pass was exciting. The driver proceeded at a break-neck, bone-rattling speed with little attention to any other traffic. At one point I asked him to stop near a huge traditional walled clan compound so that I could take a picture. I was barely able to do so when the horrified driver jumped out of the car and pushed me back into my seat, slamming the car door behind me. He explained it was possible that some women were present in the distance (there were none) in which case we would get shot at and my camera would be confiscated. The other stop on the way was more benign. The driver got out of the car, spread a carpet on the side of the road and started to pray and bow in the direction of Mecca. The hour for one of his five daily prayer rituals had come. The road to the Pass and the Pass itself form part of a rugged barren mountain landscape. As much as I enjoyed the outing, I was glad to get back alive!

As surprising and exciting as all my trips were, they do not compare in any way with my dangerous adventure in East Pakistan, when I was caught in the middle of the revolution, as described in Appendix I. Often, after my return from the country, I was asked if I had been aware of any activity related to Pakistan's nuclear bomb program during my stay there. I was not, even though, very probably, the program was just getting off the ground at that time. With the passage of time, I have considered the issue and recount briefly in Appendix II what I believe to be the history of the Pakistani nuclear effort.

In early April 1971, I left Pakistan, continuing my trip around the world bound for Kabul, the Capital of Afghanistan. Today, as I look back at my time in Pakistan, I realize though I have returned to India many times, I never again ventured to Pakistan, a country as troubled as it is wonderful. Thus, there is a sense of finality about my trip there that comes to mind from time to time. My departure from Pakistan also marked the beginning of my return journey to Oak Ridge, and I share stories about that last segment of my trip around the world next.

Around the World in 80-Plus Days – III Journey from Pakistan

My first stop after leaving Rawalpindi was Kabul. It was April 1971, prior to Russia's invasion of Afghanistan and before the current long-term U. S. entanglement in the country. At that time Afghanistan was a peaceful and fascinating place. Except for a few official buildings, palaces and mosques, all structures consisted of a form of grayish-brown color adobe. In many places the actual adobe bricks were visible, either because the protective mud plaster layer had washed away or because it was never applied in the first place. The layout of the town was conspicuous for the total absence of any planning. Tightly-packed buildings were scattered around, as though the result of dice of various sizes thrown by a careless gambler.

The kaleidoscope has saved many vibrant images from this visit. A group of street urchins staring at me in wonder and curiosity; many groups of turban-headed men sitting in a large square in front of a mosque; a young boy proudly posing for me in his "Sunday best"; a dead-end alley with a jumble of assorted windows and an open sewer; a long narrow street filled with a river of bobbing turbans; a proud tea-vendor sitting in front of two giant samovars, large versions of the one I bought in Rawalpindi and still treasure; a man and a burka-clad woman haggling in an open-air market; a "camel-exchange" reflected in huge puddles of rain water; a view from a hilltop of a cemetery with its white-lidded above-ground sarcophagi; an old man carrying a huge goat-skin container full of water; and two burka-clad ladies, sitting on the edge of a river and, no doubt, gossiping.

Socializing in Kabul, Capital of Afghanistan

From Kabul I flew to Istanbul. In the Kabul airport, I had one of my treasures confiscated. It was a head, carved from stone, of a warrior purported to be from the time when Alexander the Great reached India via what is now Afghanistan. I bought it in Pakistan from a street-vendor for a few rupees. I did not care whether it was authentic or fake. The Afghan authorities claimed that it might be a national treasure and that, as such, it could not be exported. They asked for my address in the U.S. and said that if the item was not a national treasure, they would return it to me. I never saw it again, and so, although I doubt it, I may have unwittingly contributed to Afghanistan's rich cultural heritage!

On the flight from Kabul to Istanbul, I sat next to a young Danish "world traveler." He said that he was in trouble because all his money was stolen in Kabul and he needed means to contact his parents and ask them to wire some funds to Istanbul for him. He said that if I lent him some cash, he would pay me back when he got home to Denmark. I gave him twenty dollars and did not expect to ever see them again. But, lo and behold, a few weeks later I was, indeed, reimbursed. The experience goes to show that "one good turn deserves another" and that one should not pre-judge people.

There is not much that needs to be said about Istanbul. It is a marvelous place, and most of the historical part has not changed much since the time I was there on my return trip from Pakistan. My final adventure during the trip came when I cleared customs on arrival in New York. With all the wonderful cheap hashish that was available everywhere in Asia, I succumbed to the temptation of smuggling some in the size and shape of a silver dollar. I concealed it in my sock, and since customs did not utilize sniffing dogs at the time, I thought my contraband would go undetected. But I also had another problem, that of excess luggage weight. To help with this, I wore a huge sheepskin Afghan jacket, long since eaten by the moths, and filled all pockets with a variety of heavy articles, including books, statuettes, etc. The pockets were noticeably bulging. As I was attempting to walk through the "nothing to declare" line, I was pulled aside and ushered into a small room, where the door closed in on me. "OK. This is it! This means prison for attempted smuggling of illicit drugs. But no! Salvation!" All that the customs gentlemen were interested in was the legal contents of the overstuffed pockets of the coat.

And so ended the saga of one of the most wonderfully exotic and dangerous trips of my life, "Around the World in 80-Plus Days."

SECTION SEVEN

Carol

I have often told the following story as a joke though it actually expresses my true feelings. I mentioned earlier that I coveted the house Bob Ferguson built from the time I first visited it and told him if he ever wanted to sell it, he should not put it on the market because I would simply buy it from him. I also believe that I fell in love with Carol the first day I saw her and was determined to marry her should she ever become available. In time, I would jokingly say that when Bob's house and Carol came on the market, I planned to acquire them both. As circumstances played out, Carol and the Ferguson house *both* actually *did so* at nearly the same time. On April 12, 1980, a year or so after her divorce, Carol and I married, and in early 1981, we moved into the Bob Ferguson's house on West Outer Drive.

Primary Home in Oak Ridge, Tennessee

Our wedding took place in the afternoon, in the garden of our home, under dogwood blossoms, with all our children in attendance: my David and Maia, then ages 24 and 9 respectively, and Carol's Amy and Steve, ages 20 and 16. The official part of the ceremony was performed by a friend of ours, who was also a justice of the peace, and the spiritual aspect was represented by a senior member of the local synagogue. At the time, my parents were living in Vienna and did not attend, mostly due to the distance involved, but also because my father, once again, did not approve of my marriage. He regarded Carol as too old for me and felt I should have chosen someone much younger. Also, although he did not say so, realizing he was anti-Semitic, I knew he did not approve of my marrying a Jew. Some one hundred guests attended our wedding, and champagne was flowing freely, to the point of my incapacitation at the end of the day. For me, this was not the best ending to a beautiful day.

I believe that Carol and I are a good match. We love and share many of the same interests: music, theatre, serious movies, and travel. We have very similar political, ethical and religious views. We both believe in healthy eating habits and in the many benefits of exercise. Carol teaches five exercise classes per week at the new Oak Ridge Senior Center and I participate in three of them. In 1981, she completed her Ph.D. at the University of Tennessee. The subject of her thesis was the scapula of the Neanderthal man, which has a ridge that is not present in modern man. In Germany, where they pay great attention to titles, she would be known as "Frau Doktor, Doktor," which means the wife of a Doctor, who is also a Doctor! We share many aspects of our lives, exchanging views which are not always in complete alignment. We considered having a child together and underwent counselling regarding this option. The therapist quickly convinced us not to do so when he said, "Why spoil a good thing?"

We went on two honeymoon trips, both potentially dangerous. The first took place soon after our wedding. I was invited to present a scientific paper at a conference in France in mid-April, 1980. Carol accompanied me on this trip, and after the conference we travelled to Geneva with the goal of skiing down from the Aiguille du Midi along the Mer de Glace. Aptly named, the Aiguille du

Midi (Needle of the South) can be reached via a spectacular two-section cable car from the French resort town of Chamonix. At 12,605 ft., it sits close to the highest peak of Western Europe, Mont Blanc (15,774 ft.). From the Aiguille, a steep and exposed ice ridge leads to a large glacier, the Mer de Glace (Sea of Ice). This glacier, the second largest in the Alps, is about 4.5 miles long and 600 ft. deep. It is crisscrossed by crevasses, which are covered by a layer of snow in the winter.

Carol

I failed to properly research our proposed skiing adventure and was not aware that at the end of April the season for skiing down the Mer de Glace was over. By that time the snow cover of the crevasses was melted, and skiers were at risk of falling into them. There was nobody at the top of the Aiguille to warn us, and we proceeded blindly with our plan. One lonely ski trace marked our way, and we were very fortunate not to end up in a crevasse. Due to the slushy nature of the melting snow, Carol fell onto her ski, skinning her nose. Having against all odds successfully reached the bottom of the Mer de Glace, the next surprise was the absence of the usual bus transportation back to Chamonix. To reach our destination, we were forced to walk several miles along a summer railroad track in our ski boots, carrying our skis and climbing over boulders. After a brief stop at the Chamonix hospital to take care of Carol's nose, we returned to Geneva, lucky to have escaped with our lives. Soon after this event, we traveled to Vienna to see my parents, who organized a gathering to introduce their new daughter-in-law to their friends. True to his nature, father gave Carol a hard time because she had a band aid on her nose, thus concealing her good looks.

Our second honeymoon took place later that year. We flew to Bolivia and planned to continue on land to Lake Titicaca, by steam ship to the floating reed islands of the Uros indigenous people, by bus to Cusco, and finally by train to the ancient concealed Inca stronghold of Machu Picchu. After a day or two in the fascinating capital of Bolivia, La Paz, on July 17, the "Junta of Commanders," headed by Garcia Meza, forced a violent coup d'état, sometimes referred to as the Cocaine Coup. As we ventured out of our hotel on to the main avenue of the city, we found bullets flying over our heads. We quickly ducked into the nearest store we could find that was not boarded up. There we found an American lady, Barbara, and her daughter, Denise, who was on a Peace Corps assignment in Paraguay.

In a day or two, after the fighting subsided somewhat, we moved from our hotel to Barbara's smaller and more secluded place. There were very few planes leaving La Paz, but since we had "open airline tickets," we were able to book a flight on a German Lufthansa flight to Santiago, the capital of Chile. Our ride to the airport was an adventure in itself. We were piled on top of a mountain of luggage on the back of a truck, dodging various things people were throwing at us, including rocks. While Denise ultimately returned to her Peace Corps post, we and Barbara were the last to get on the Lufthansa plane. On landing in Santiago, which was at that time under the control of the brutal dictator Augusto Pinochet, we nevertheless breathed a breath of "freedom." To celebrate, we got "pissed on pisco sours." We remained close friends with Barbara until her untimely death from cancer several years later.

My deepest regret in my relationship with Carol is the misery I caused her with my ever-increasing alcoholism. Early in our relationship, my drinking was under control, although I fixed myself a stiff margarita as soon as I got home from work. In time, I mixed two margaritas for myself. Thus, my drinking continued to increase as time passed. When under the influence, I was mean to Carol, something that I will never forgive myself for. My drinking increased with Maia's difficult teen years and zoomed up exponentially when my beloved Maia died. I crashed and became a classic alcoholic. There were DUI arrests, usually mitigated by skilled and expensive lawyers. I spent a number of days in jail and a month in a residential rehabilitation institution on two different occasions. As I write this, I am sober, with a promise to myself, and to Carol, to remain so for the rest of my life.

Return to Geneva, Switzerland and to Brookhaven, New York

With my thoughts shifting to Geneva, I'm reminded of Heraclitus, whom I quoted earlier, for wisely stating, "No man ever steps in the same river twice, for it is not the same river and he's not the same man." Such **is** the case with my return to Geneva, Switzerland, to work on the WA80 experiment. Without doubt, on a personal level, that assignment was the most enjoyable period of my research career. Several reasons explain this opinion. First, the other four group leaders working on this research effort and I had associated with each other at earlier points in time, often working on the same research projects. These previous experiences had created a culture of trust and team effort among us, as opposed to the competition that often pervades the atmosphere in large collaborations. Second, we undertook a project that was challenging in an area in which we lacked experience of any kind: nucleus-nucleus collisions at ultra-relativistic energies.

With skepticism, our colleagues regarded us as inexperienced "amateurs." We interpreted this perception as a challenge and therefore vigorously undertook the goal to prove them wrong **and** ourselves as far more than rookies!

We designed and constructed the WA80 experiment from scratch at CERN, the European Organization for Nuclear Research, located in Geneva, Switzerland. The scientific goal was to re-create a state in which the entire universe may have existed a few instants after the Big Bang of creation: the Quark-Gluon Plasma (QGP). Let me explain. As most readers know, nuclei of atoms are made up of protons and neutrons. These protons and neutrons, collectively known as nucleons, can exist on their own as individual entities. Nucleons, in turn, are made up of three quarks held together by massless particles called gluons ("the glue that hold the quarks together"). However, unlike the nucleons, we have not been able to isolate quarks. The energy required to break a quark loose from its confinement appears to be infinite. But calculations indicate that at sufficiently large temperatures and pressures, (sufficiently large energy density), the confinement of quarks can be broken, and the quarks and gluons are free to roam forming a kind of a "soup," referred to as the Quark-Gluon Plasma. The calculations also indicate that these extreme temperatures and pressures could be achieved by means of the CERN accelerators.

CERN is home to a large number of accelerators, some of which operate in tandem, yielding projectiles of various energies. Our experiments made use of the SPS (Super Proton Synchrotron), which at the start of our experiment produced accelerated oxygen nuclei with energies of 60 and 200 billion electron volts per nucleon (60 A GeV and 200 A GeV). This can be compared to energies in the range of millions of electron volts (MeV) at which all my earlier experimental investigations were carried out. Our Oak Ridge group skipped a large research area associated with energies in the range of 1 to 5 billion electron volts, making our learning curve very steep. The name WA80 derives simply from being the 80th experiment in the West Area of the SPS. Between 40 and 50 researchers were involved in the endeavor at any given time. I am coauthor of 25 WA80 refereed journal articles, 17 refereed conference proceedings, and 40 conference proceedings not refereed. I also gave 12 presentations at conferences in as many countries. WA80 was succeeded by WA98 and projectiles as heavy as lead became available. This research resulted in 23 journal articles, 15 refereed conference proceedings and 3 conference proceedings not refereed. By all measures, the experiments in the SPS West Area were very productive. The WA80 experiments were initiated in November 1986, and in January 1987 I presented very preliminary results at a conference in Bormio, Italy. Our experiments at CERN were carried out over a period of about 17 years, and during this time we learned a great deal about the systematics of nucleus-nucleus collisions at ultra-relativistic energies. Given our achievements and contributions to science, we were no longer considered clueless amateurs. While we did not find any evidence for the "Holy Grail" of QGP formation, we accumulated extensive data to which results from future reactions at higher temperatures and pressures would be compared in the effort to eliminate background events.

My personal life in Geneva was very pleasant. We worked at CERN typically 5 to 6 weeks at a time. On occasions when Carol could not join me because of work, I would stay at one of the CERN dormitories. The accommodations were somewhat Spartan, with showers in the single rooms and toilets in the hallways. I was much happier when Carol joined me. On days off, we would make short excursions to the Alps or other surrounding areas. I remember one Thanksgiving Day when we found ourselves in the Rhone valley with our friends Bob Ferguson and his wife eating a specialty cheese fondue into which potatoes rather than bread were dipped. One summer Maia joined us and got together with our friends' daughters who were close to her in age. Alone or with Carol, I went skiing in winter, boating in summer, explored the countryside in spring and fall, and visited friends from the old days in all seasons.

A series of conferences was dedicated to the possibility of QGP formation. Their title was "International Conference on Ultra-Relativistic Nucleus-Nucleus Collisions." The Oak Ridge National Laboratory (ORNL) was selected to host the 9th conference in the series, November 11 – 15, 1991, in the nearby resort town of Gatlinburg, Tennessee. I was Chairman of the

Conference, colloquially referred to as "Quark Matter '91." More than 360 participants from 27 countries, which was about 100 participants more than at any other conference in the series, attended the event indicating a growing interest in the field. I learned that the organization of such a large conference is a full-time job for a better part of a year, even with the support of an excellent local Organizing Committee and an active International Advisory Committee. I felt gratified when I was told that we set a new and higher standard for the conference series. The 669-page proceedings of the conference, edited by me and four ORNL colleagues, were published as a special edition of the "Nuclear Physics" journal by North Holland.

There was an interesting episode associated with the organization of the conference, indicating the type of political problem that one can unwittingly stumble into. As Conference Chairman, together with the advice of the International Advisory Committee, I was tasked with selecting a number of keynote speakers, covering topics such as the Experimental Overview, the Theoretical Overview, and Concluding Remarks. A famous German theoretical physicist, Walter Greiner, visited ORNL some months before the Quark Matter '91 conference and stopped by to give me some unsolicited advice. He made it clear that he would like to be one of the keynote speakers. He was qualified in terms of his standing in the physics community, but had not been very involved in the ultra-relativistic regime. I politely told him that I would be making my selection with the advice of the International Committee. I then asked him, hypothetically I thought, were the Advisory Committee recommend that he present the Concluding Remarks, would he be willing to do so? He enthusiastically said "yes."

In the past, concluding remarks were presented by theorists. However, with the input of the Advisory Committee, we decided to have them presented by an experimentalist and, as it turned out, no friend of Greiner. I received a phone call from one of Greiner's colleagues, asking me what I had done because Greiner was walking up and down the hallways, cursing me and saying I had double-crossed him. Evidently, with my asking about his availability, he considered his invitation to be "a done deal." I wrote a long and polite letter to Greiner, explaining how the misunderstanding had arisen. He replied in a note I still treasure: "Your many words mean nothing! Boil in your own juice!!" It took many years before he forgave me and invited me to present a talk at a conference in his honor in South Africa.

Even before completion of the CERN experiments, we started to plan experiments at Brookhaven National Laboratory's (BNL) Relativistic Heavy Ion Collider (RHIC). The quote about the "not the same river" and "not the same man" is once again pertinent. I left BNL in 1967 as a young physicist for a research staff position at ORNL and was returning some 30 years later as a well-established Section Head in ORNL's Physics Division to work on one of the two large experiments at RHIC. This accelerator was designed to produce much larger energy densities (combination of pressure and temperature) than those available at CERN. Thus, the probability of creating the QGP was much higher at BNL than it had been at CERN. The main reason for RHIC's ability to produce higher energy densities is that, as its name states, it is a collider. Instead of accelerated nuclei colliding with stationary nuclei, the ions in a collider circulate in opposite directions and are made to collide in what are known as "intersection regions," in which the various experiments are located. Everything at RHIC was scaled up about an order of magnitude, relative to the experiments at CERN's SPS. The number of people involved in each of the two large experiments, STAR and PHENIX, was approximately 500 physicists and as many engineers. The size of the experimental equipment was also proportionately larger. This was definitely "Big Physics!"

Our ORNL group joined the PHENIX experiment, with Shoji Nagamiya from Columbia as the initial spokesman. In the early stages of PHENIX, I was part of a six-member Executive Committee and had significant influence over the planning and execution of the experiment. However, some management changes were implemented on the departure of Nagamiya for his native Japan. I was not happy with the outcome. Data taking started in 2000, and preliminary data were reported at the Quark Matter 2001 conference in January on Long Island, N.Y. In time, PHENIX, as expected, was very productive. My name appeared in 55 refereed articles, 59 refereed conference proceedings and 28 proceedings, not refereed.[7] Due to the heavy competition for presentation of results at conferences, I had no speaking engagements on behalf of PHENIX. My final assignment was to head up a 3-member Speakers Committee. Our task was to decide which PHENIX members were to give talks at various conferences. This was a "lose – lose" job. We were constantly being lobbied by various Group Leaders on behalf of their associates, or themselves. On some occasions we had trouble reaching consensus within our committee. Given this difficult PHENIX job, and the fact that experimental results were slow in coming, my attitude regarding the PHENIX enterprise started to sour.

Around this time, ORNL's Physics Division experienced a funding problem, which led to my retirement about two years earlier than I had planned. Previously, as section head, I hired two young physicists, and now I had to face the prospect of letting them go. On the other hand, if I were to retire, both could be kept on. This is what I decided to do. But other events also influenced my decision. I got into an argument with the Department of Energy funding agent associated with one of my groups. Unfortunately, my Division Director did not back me up and, even worse, he demoted me to Group Leader. Unrelated to these events, but executed as if meant to compensate for them, I was appointed "Corporate Fellow" in 1999. This position is the

---

7   Refer to Appendix III, "A Note Regarding Scientific Publications," for my view on how to measure scientific output.

highest rung on ORNL's non-management research ladder, one that involves a significant increase in salary. Taking everything into consideration, I resigned as Group Leader by handing the job over to my very able colleague, Glenn Young, and made preparations to retire on January 1, 2002, at the age of 63, about two years earlier than I had intended. Thus ended my long and varied scientific career, my only immediate regret being that I enjoyed the Corporate Fellow's salary for little more than a year.

The bottom line: at the time of my retirement, the Quark-Gluon Plasma had not been detected in the laboratory.

The Tragedy of Maia

Earlier, I paused the story of my beloved Maia at the point when in 1985, at the age of 14, she was admitted, against her will, to a psychiatric hospital and the kaleidoscope turned black. After her release, Maia spent many years struggling with drug addiction. I offered to help her whenever I could, but only occasionally would she allow me to do so. The kaleidoscope flickered during that period, but mostly with gray images. For various reasons Maia was expelled from Oak Ridge High School, and we arranged for her to attend a private liberal school in Knoxville. She graduated and continued her studies at a community college earning an associate degree despite her continued drug use and engagement in a number of promiscuous relationships. In the early nineties, Maia appeared to have gotten her life together. She married a wonderful young man, Jamie Parkey, and, on July 19, 1992, their daughter Amira was born. Unfortunately, the marriage did not last, and Maia resumed her self-destructive ways. At one point she married a cross-dressing illegal Mexican immigrant, Carlos, who pursued her for the sole purpose of obtaining a green card. When it became clear that he was abusing Amira, Maia had the strength to force him to leave.

In 2004, Maia was admitted to an in-house treatment center in Michigan's Upper Peninsula. Unfortunately, that facility turned out to be run by fundamentalist fanatics who treated the center like a prison and regarded "patients" as indentured servants, held against their will. Thankfully, Maia managed to escape and return by bus to Knoxville. I was not in Oak Ridge at the time, and she ended up camping in the back yard of a friend, Alfred, with whom she ultimately started a romantic relationship and eventually married, well after the turmoil and aftermath of her earlier marriages. I sensed that Alfred was deeply in love with Maia and fully devoted to her. Carol did not, however, share my view.

On the morning of February 26, 2008, at about 8:00, Carol and I received an unexpected phone call. Alfred, Maia's husband, was on the line and barely coherent. Between sobs, he was able to communicate that he woke up that morning to find Maia lying dead beside him. To this day, it remains a mystery of nature to me as to how, though completely unprepared, I could experience such a thunder bolt and continue to breathe and live. In my mind, only one possible explanation exists. Stunned by the shock, my intellect gropingly gathered the words. The power to realize their *full* intent was mercifully absent. My mind had a nonsensical impression of a vast loss and that is all. I knew I would need years to gather the details and thus know as well as understand the full extent of my loss....

Suddenly, a bright kaleidoscope image entered my thoughts. It was one of a small baby girl, on the day of her birth, June 6, 1971, in the arms of my smiling mother. As soon as the image appeared, it vanished.

I remember the rest of that day, and the days that followed, through an alcoholic haze. With Carol driving, we rushed to Alfred and Maia's home, a rustic house in the woods I had bought and placed at their disposal. The police had arrived and were already removing Maia in a sealed body bag. Officials had designated the site a potential crime scene, and I was not allowed to see her. Since I was in no condition to deal with any detail of what had occurred in the subsequent days, my son David took charge.

David

He meant well yet moved so quickly. He had Maia cremated before I had a chance to see her. Perhaps his decision was for the best, but at the time it only added to my agony. Another casualty was the disappearance of the jewelry, including a valuable heirloom diamond ring, that Maia was wearing at the time of her death. Sifting her ashes showed no traces of any items, and helpful detectives could not solve the puzzle. With time, I came to accept probable theft, which was trivial compared to the real loss.

Then another bright image appeared: I am holding my four-year-old Maia by the hand, and she is looking up adoringly at me. Again, just a brief flicker….

Maia and Myself

Maia's death certificate listed the cause of her death as "hydrocodone, quetiapine and citalopram intoxication." Verbally, the medical examiner told me she regarded the cause of death to be an accidental overdose of these drugs. Hydrocodone is a pain-relieving narcotic, quetiapine is an antipsychotic drug used to treat bipolar disorder, and citalopram is an antidepressant.

Whether any of these drugs were obtained through legal prescriptions remained unclear. The death certificate also cited "other significant conditions contributing to death...recent oxycodone use and bronchial asthma." Maia was morbidly obese at the time of her death, and given her asthma condition, she often had trouble breathing. During the night of February 26, at about 2:00 a.m., her breathing stopped, and she died peacefully in her sleep. The day before her death, Maia spent a pleasant sunny and warm late February afternoon with Alfred in their wooded backyard. Looking forward to it, they talked about plans for the next day. These details eliminated any fleeting thoughts that the overdose of drugs was deliberate.

In due course, a memorial service was organized at Maia's neighborhood church. I regret that I was intoxicated when I attended it, and I regret even more that I did not remain silent. Maia was deeply religious, and the minister talked about "a better place" and "being reunited there with her loved ones." Rising, I said with tears streaming down my face that I wished I could believe her message because it would ease the pain, but that I was not able to do so. Later that summer, David organized a touching event at our Lakehouse. A Viking ship carrying some of Maia's ashes was sent off ablaze into the night. I still have some of her ashes and maintain a small discreet shrine in her honor in a closet at home. I quietly remember and celebrate all her various anniversaries and milestones, and she lives in my heart every day.

The Time has Come...

Lewis Carroll famously wrote: "The time has come," the walrus said, "to talk of many things: of shoes and ships - and sealing wax - of cabbages and kings." And so, in wrapping up this memoir, the time has indeed come for me to talk of many things, but I will skip shoes, ships, sealing wax, cabbages, and even kings. I have learned a lot about myself in the process of putting pen on paper (or rather fingers on the computer keyboard) to compose this memoir. I note that some kaleidoscope images shine brighter than I remember them before starting out; others, regrettably, became even duller than they were in the past. The images that lack luster reflect my realization that I did not always handle life's situations as well as I thought I had before getting my stories on paper and reflecting on them with objectivity. My interaction with my adopted son David, when he was little, offers one strong example of this insight. Details about us that came to mind as I wrote were both illuminating and revealing, making me realize how

Godric

Amira and David

surprisingly therapeutic the writing process can be. I lifted painful issues or events off my chest by writing, ending years of preoccupation from my heart. At times, the experience made me feel as though I was making amends for wrongs I might have done. Whenever I started to describe some painful event, I had no understanding as to how helpful the process would be. Without doubt, the single most therapeutic experience was writing about Maia's death. I could never have anticipated the depth of the emotional release it provided.

In retrospect, the facets of my life that hold the greatest importance for me personally are my legacies, which fall into two categories: professional and family. I am proud that I had a role in the hiring of Glenn Young, and equally proud about bringing Soren Sorensen to Tennessee. Both have contributed in many ways to physics in general, and to the Oak Ridge National Laboratory (ORNL) and the University of Tennessee (UT) in particular. I discussed their many contributions earlier, and it was with great satisfaction that I saw Soren advance to the position of Head of the UT Department of Physics and Astronomy and serve in that capacity for many years and Glenn lead ORNL's Physics Division as Director for part of his illustrious career. Another example is that of Geoffrey Greene, who received the 2020 American Physical Society's Bonner Prize. I congratulated him and in reply, he expressed his appreciation for my persuading him to come to UT/ORNL and generously added that he doubts he would have received the award without my help. There have been others, either UT faculty members and/or ORNL research staff members, whom I either hired initially, or enticed to settle in Tennessee. Noteworthy is the addition of Vince Cianciolo as a permanent member of our group in 1997. He is one of the most versatile and imaginative scientists that I have ever known. He and his wife Maureen have become our treasured friends, and we were happy to have shared many fun days with them and their lively four boys at their house and at our Lakehouse. I was also reminded recently by Tom Davies, a former member of the Theoretical Group of ORNL's Physics Division, that I turned his professional life around by simply suggesting he spend some time as a visitor at the Los Alamos National Laboratory. These noteworthy accomplishments reflect my personal efforts and influence, giving me the greatest satisfaction.

Archer

I have written about many family members earlier, but here I want to single out those to whom I feel the closest, in addition to my wife, Carol. By this, I mean close both emotionally and physically. They are Carol's son Steven Dittner and his wife Cindy, and my granddaughter Amira Lawson, and her children Godric and Archer. Steven and Cindy live in Oak Ridge, and we call on them often when we need help. Cindy is a native of the mountains of East Tennessee, a true "coalminer's daughter." Contrary to the stereotypes, she is extremely intelligent. She is also gentle, considerate, and very helpful. Steve I love like my son, and I believe this feeling is mutual. Steve has many passions. The latest are physical competitions such as "Ironman" and service on various Oak Ridge City Environmental Boards. His help with our Oak Ridge house, the Lakehouse, and the two power boats we own is invaluable. They have two children, Madison and Brian, both adults on their way to productive careers. Other members of Carol's family include her daughter, Amy Wenke and husband Steven. They have two children by Amy's earlier marriage, Victoria and Jaqueline Morris. We treasure a wonderful photograph from a long-ago gathering of the whole clan at the Lakehouse, including a very young Amira.

Family gathering, Carol, Steve, Cindy, Amira, Archer and Godric

**At the Lakehouse, Steven and Amy Wenke,
Cindy and Steve, Brian, Carol and Myself,
Jaqueline, Victoria, Amira, and Madison**

Amira, Maia's daughter, understandably experienced a rough time following her mother's unexpected death in 2008. After exploring various career and study options, on July 24, 2010, she married a young man, Jacob Lawson. Their first child, Godric, was born on September 23, 2010, followed by a beautiful little girl, Archer, born on Carol's and my 33rd wedding anniversary, April 12, 2013. As I write this, Amira works with her father, Jamie Parkey, installing or refinishing hardwood floors. Amira is an exemplary mother, instilling in her children values such as consideration and politeness. Amira and her family are the joy of my existence and a consolation prize for the loss of Maia. They live in Knoxville in a small house I bought for them and we talk to them and see them often. The kaleidoscope radiates with beautiful pictures of Amira's wedding and of Godric and Archer on many occasions, as they grow up.

The kaleidoscope insists that I recount the story of "The Three Musketeers," Ray Nix, Bill Myers, and myself. That was what we called ourselves at the height of what we assumed to be an everlasting friendship. We vacationed together, went on skiing and sailing trips, and attended scientific meetings together. We had been graduate students together at Berkeley, Ray and Bill in the Theoretical Physics Division and I in an experimental group of the Chemistry Division. And then, on a sailing trip off the coast of Turkey, the friendship was shattered forever. At the time, six of us were sailing our own chartered boat—Ray, who was the skipper in charge of the boat and his wife Sally; Bill, his wife Valerie; and Carol and me. We cruised along the Turkish coast from west to east. During the first part of the trip, there were several incidents which led to a strained relationship between Ray and Bill and Valerie. On top of that, even though Bill had extensive sailing experience, Ray told him that he, Ray, was not comfortable when Bill was at helm and asked him to stop taking the wheel. Since the ladies were not officially qualified, only Ray and I took turns piloting the craft. On our return, a huge storm sprang up, with waves so high that the boat disappeared in their valleys. The ladies went below deck and were frightened, and Bill and

I were very concerned. As it happened, we were near a Greek island, where we had stopped earlier when outward-bound. The direction of the raging wind would have made it easy for us to simply head for the island and 'hole up" there. Everybody, except Ray, was in favor of doing so. Using the skipper's prerogative, Ray insisted that we continue our original course and take shelter behind an uninhabited island some distance away. With my help, he tried several maneuvers in an attempt to set the appropriate course. However, the direction of the gale made it impossible for any of them to succeed. In the end, we limped into the Greek port, stayed overnight, and woke up to calm weather and a warm breakfast. Bill would never speak to Ray again. I was caught, very uncomfortably, in the middle yet remained friends with both. While Ray died some time ago, I maintain my friendship with Bill to this day.

The kaleidoscope also glows with images of close friends nudging me for a place in this memoir. I have already mentioned two of them, Phillip Armitage who sent me copies of Queen Mary College lectures while I was stuck in a wheelchair in Geneva following my accident in the summer of 1958, and Robin Penberthy, whom I mentioned in connection with an incident on my arrival in Tokyo in 1971. Robin is a life-long friend from my days at the International School in Geneva, and I have maintained contact with him to this day. We have seen him and his wife Anne on a number of occasions in recent years during our visits to London. They live in a beautiful penthouse apartment near Hampstead

Heath, and we even stayed with them on one occasion. I got to know Phillip somewhat later during my undergraduate days in London, but he has also remained a life-long friend. I last saw him in the fall of 2017, when Carol and I visited him and his wife Mary in their beautiful Hindlip Manor near Worcester, which they saved from ruin by restoring it to its original beauty.

The kaleidoscope continues nudging, this time reminding me of our French family. I first met Francoise Pougheon, who is a nuclear physicist, at a scientific meeting in 1977 in Bormio, Italy. Little did I know that the event would lead to a life-long friendship between our two families on many levels. The kaleidoscope shows images of family events such as weddings; Carol and I being honored as Americans on the French "Bastille Day" in the small village, Landricourt, in which the Pougheons have a family country home predating World War I; the agony of the unexpected death of Francois, the husband of Francoise, while in Spain on vacation; a huge family reunion in Landricourt with many children and grandchildren; relaxing after a super meal, featuring braised rabbit, in their beautiful apartment in Bourg-la-Reine, a suburb of Paris; exploring museums and other sights in Paris with Francoise and then enjoying a Greek dinner with her in the Latin Quarter; Carol, Francoise and I touring Tunisia and visiting the parents of Francoise's daughter-in-law; all of Carol's children and grandchildren, having invaded Landricourt, waiting for the morning bakery truck; F. and F. relaxing at our lake house in Tennessee;

returning slowly with Francoise from a scientific meeting via a scenic route; and many, many more bright kaleidoscope pictures.

Finally, the kaleidoscope makes sure that images of Bonnie Carroll and Roy Cooper are included. They are our best friends, and when they are in town we often get together on the spur of the moment. I have known Bonnie from the time I moved to Oak Ridge, admiring her bright intellect and radiant physical beauty. I watched with awe the twists and turns of her professional career, starting out as a staff member at ORNL and ultimately creating a company centered around scientific and technical information and data, with more than two hundred and fifty employees located in Washington, D.C. and Oak Ridge. Carol and I knew Roy Cooper, Bonnie's husband-to-be, from the time he was a staff member at ORNL, and we were delighted

Françoise Pougheon

Bonnie Carroll

that they decided to get married the same year that Carol and I did. We were married on April 12, 1980 and Bonnie and Roy on July 4. As part of their wedding ceremony, I was asked to "keep an eye" on them annually by holding a sort of "State of the Union" discussion with them. We kept up this formality for a number of years until it was clear to all of us that their union, like ours, was healthy and durable. We will treasure this close friendship for the rest of our days.

Now, in closing, the kaleidoscope reverberates with the brilliant music and words of the inspirational Beethoven's 9th Symphony, "Ode to Joy." The last movement glorifies the virtue of friendship and proclaims: "all men will become brothers." This is my good fortune. The gift of so many strong friendships and family ties, which form the bedrock of my existence. And so, with joy and gratitude, I end this narrative.

Appendix I
Incident in Pakistan or, Fission: Nuclear and National[8]
By Frank Plasil

Our microbus rattled at high speed down the dusty country road. It shook violently as it occasionally darted onto the rutted shoulder to avoid an oxcart or a camel. We had left Rawalpindi, and now we fought our way against the stream of workers headed for the city on bicycles, in horse-drawn tongas, and in overcrowded buses. The other scientists and I sat silently and watched with sleepy eyes the mud houses of the villages flying past. It was my first trip to the Pakistan Institute of Science and Technology (PINSTECH), located in the middle of nowhere, about 20 miles from Islamabad, the capital. The road passed through an undulating, heavily eroded countryside. There were few trees, and the harshness of the brown dust was relieved by patches of fresh green wheat and by the startling yellow of the mustard fields. In the distance were the foothills of the Himalayas. Behind a bend against the backdrop of the

---

8   Plasil, Frank, "Incident in Pakistan, or" *ORNL Review Magazine* Vol 5, No.1, (1971). Reformatted Reprint.

Punjab hills I caught a glimpse of PINSTECH. Its white splendor was like a modern Taj Mahal: a veritable temple of science. I was startled, even though I had been prepared for the sight. PINSTECH was to be my home for the next two months. I had arrived to try to perform a fission experiment with the 5-MW reactor, which is housed in a beautiful white and gold dome, surrounded by a fountain-studded reflecting pool. My visit was part of the Sister Laboratory arrangement between Pakistan AEC and Oak Ridge National Laboratory, funded by the U.S. Agency for International Development (AID).

Pakistan is a country with limited power resources and is setting out on the road to industrialization. It is a country with a good use for nuclear energy. It has one nuclear power station almost completed near Karachi, and another one planned for East Pakistan. This is the reason for the existence of PINSTECH, and also for the Sister Laboratory program. A small reactor can serve as a training ground for engineers needed to staff the power reactors. Research on the small reactor can support a group of nuclear scientists who are familiar with reactor problems and can in turn provide fruitful interaction with engineers. Together they can form a small center of nuclear know-how. Basic reactor-oriented research in a developing country can be very relevant to international development and thus a legitimate recipient of AID funds. I won't try to describe all the aspects of the Sister Laboratory arrangement. The program is administered at ORNL by Lewis Nelson of the Director's Division, H. W. Schmitt of the Physics

Division, and M. K. Wilkinson of Solid State Division. Among its activities is training Pakistani scientists in reactor-oriented research at ORNL and sending ORNL scientists to Pakistan to help them begin their own independent research. A recent visitor from Pakistan under this program was G. Dastgir Alam, who worked in our fission group in the Physics Division for 15 months, returning to PINSTECH in September 1970.

Our microbus stopped at the back entrance in front of a red carpet lined with potted flowers and palms. The welcome, it turned out, was not for me. The prime minister of Mauritius had visited the place a few days earlier. The back entrance was used because the front entrance, which is to be graced by a modern version of a Moghul water garden, was not yet finished. We were invited to inspect the institute. It consists of a two-story concrete canopy of graceful lines forming four sides of a quadrangle. In the center will be a garden, patterned after the famous Shalimar garden at Lahore. Under the canopy, the buildings, all in the same style, line the edges of the garden on three sides of the quadrangle. The fourth side is open, revealing a view across the countryside to Rawalpindi; the reactor dome itself stands in its reflecting pool near the opposite side of the quadrangle. The exhaust stack, also gilded, stands at a discreet distance from the dome in the same reflecting pool. The dome, an obvious target, was covered with mud during the Indo-Pakistani war of 1965. It has never lost the scars of that camouflage. Most of the buildings are not yet complete, and our footsteps echoed as we walked through them. Although the laboratory will someday employ 1,000 people, at this time, only the building near the reactor was occupied, and total employment stood at about 200. We passed through air-lock doors into the reactor dome, wearing white overshoes of the type that tourists sometimes wear when they visit a mosque. The floor of the reactor hall was, in fact, not unlike a holy place. It was clean, uncluttered, and quiet-an excellent place for contemplation; the reactor was down.

Within one week the serenity was gone. A team of Polish engineers arrived to install a neutron diffraction spectrometer, and our fission experiment was getting off the ground, generating a frenetic activity of the kind we Western physicists found more normal. The experiment we planned had been agreed on before my arrival. The idea was to compare fission fragment distributions obtained from resonance neutron-induced fission of plutonium-239 with distributions obtained from thermal-neutron-induced fission of plutonium-239. The distributions were to be obtained by measuring energies of both fission fragments from fission events in each of the two cases. I brought with me the solid-state detectors used to measure fragment energies, and a zinc crystal used to select neutrons of the required energy by diffraction techniques. I also brought with me a variety of experimental odds and ends and felt relieved that I had not been put to explain them in customs searches in Katmandu and Varanasi.

The next few weeks were a drama of persistence.

Dastgir Alam and I, with our several helpers ranging from janitors (referred to, widely, as "peons") to junior scientists, battled overwhelming odds. Our techniques ranged from Boy Scout-style self-help to cunning, from pleading to browbeating. "Let's move that beam stop," I would say. The answer might be, "Yes, we will on Monday." "I meant today," I would counter. "Fine, after lunch and the Friday prayer period at about 2 PM." "NOW!" Sometimes it worked.

Our first task was to map out the reactor beam and to install a rotating platform to hold the crystal and the fission chamber. Next came orientation of the crystal, and identification of the refracting planes. This enabled us to obtain a diffracted neutron beam of the same energy as the plutonium-239 resonance. At this point we found that the construction of the fission chamber was proceeding at a rate that would complete the job in a little over a year. We took the matter into our own hands. Starting from scratch, we built a simple vacuum-tight chamber in four days. This was possible by our continuous physical presence in the machine shop where we worked alongside three machinists. There was no fear of union grievances, and all were impressed by the crazy pair of Ph.D.s actually working lathes and drilling holes. All that remained before the actual experiment was the stacking of shielding, assembling of the electronic gear, and testing of the detectors.

Every day our senior scientist microbus delivered us to the laboratory at 8 AM, after a one-hour ride. The next hour or so was spent drinking tea, discussing the news, waiting for the air conditioning (or heating) to be turned on and the reactor to be brought up. The highlight of the day came at noon when half a dozen of us would crowd around a small table in our joint office and wait for the janitor to bring our food. My lunch came from the mess hall; others brought food from home. All the reheated curries were placed in the center of the table. Eating with our hands, we helped ourselves from any and all of the dishes. The food was excellent. It occurred to me the ORNL cafeteria might experiment a little with curry. At 3:30 PM everything was turned off, including the reactor, and at 4:15 we headed back to Rawalpindi.

I spent the evenings roaming about the bazaars on a rented bicycle, eating mutton kebabs and tikkas from the street vendors. I was the subject of great curiosity. Perhaps my place was really in a chauffeur-driven, air-conditioned AID limousine, avoiding crowded areas, or in the dining room of the Hotel Intercontinental. Weekends were something to look forward to. They brought such adventures as falcon hunting, a visit to the tribal areas of the historic Khyber Pass, a wedding ceremony at which the bride was never seen by male guests, getting snowbound in the mountains when the temperature in Rawalpindi was 95°F, camel rides, flying past Nanga Parbat, nearly 27,000 feet high, and watching water buffaloes bulldoze their way through crowds in narrow streets of the old city in Lahore.

The most exciting event was an extended weekend trip I took to Dacca, the capital of East Pakistan in Bengal.

To understand what happened, some political background is necessary. Pakistan is ruled under martial law by President Yahya Khan. He decided to return power to the people and declared free elections. These were orderly, but everybody was in for a surprise. When the results were announced, West Pakistan had given a majority of its votes to the Pakistan Peoples Party led by a wealthy pro-Communist, anti-American landowner called Bhutto. East Pakistan, in a show of surprising unity, was completely carried by the Awami League led by the somewhat pro-American Sheik Mujibur "Mujib" Rahman. East Pakistan has been politically dominated for many years by West Pakistan. For example, of the fifty generals in the army, only one is from East Pakistan. The Awami League won on a platform of autonomy for East Pakistan, which has 70 million inhabitants to West Pakistan's 50 million. Mujib had a clear majority, and the convening of the National Assembly to draft a constitution was set for March 3. On February 27 I arrived in East Pakistan to spend a weekend with friends in Chittagong, and to visit the AEC research laboratory in Dacca. March 1 was a Monday, and I had spent the morning visiting the Dacca Research Center. After a splendid lunch, I was about to leave a downtown restaurant with my host. We found the exit blocked, and customers and employees were peering anxiously through cracks in closed shutters. Outside, people were streaming past, carrying sticks and shouting. They poured out from a cricket stadium where a game had been interrupted by the announcement that the president, bowing to a threat by Bhutto to set West

Pakistan ablaze from Khyber to Karachi if the National Assembly were held, decided to postpone the session.

This was a blow to East Pakistanis, and crowds headed for their leader's house. In the confusion, we blended into the crowd and made our way to the Research Center. It was barricaded, and the employees were headed home. After some embarrassment about what to do with a foreign visitor, my hosts loaded me onto a Jeep which took me to the Center's guest house near the airport. I found it deserted and decided to walk to the airport and inquire about flights to West Pakistan. The airline staff said they had no news and could not get in touch with the town office. They suggested I avoid the center of town, but curiosity won out, and by means of a scooter rickshaw I headed for the airline office downtown. Only small groups of people with sticks milled about the main intersections in town, but there was a large crowd outside the Pakistan International Airline (PIA) office. The windows were smashed, desks turned over, and the office was ransacked and deserted except for a few policemen. Apparently, PIA was a symbol of West Pakistan's supremacy. I learned that a general strike had been declared for the next three days and decided that no further purpose could be served by staying in East Pakistan.

At about 10 PM I headed for the airport again. The situation there had deteriorated. Lights were off, no PIA officials were to be seen, and a crowd consisting mainly of West Pakistanis milled about the lobby. The access to the runway was guarded by soldiers, and the runway itself was lit by kerosene lamps. A PIA Boeing 707 arrived from Karachi. A military cordon went up around the plane several hundred feet from the terminal. Bewildered passengers deplaned in confusion. I was told that the plane would return without passengers. Then I noticed that some important looking officials were taking some luggage to the plane. On their next trip I joined them, pretending to be one of them, carrying my bag confidently. We were stopped by soldiers a few times, and in my best colonial arrogance (so easy to acquire) I told those who stopped us that I had nothing to discuss with them, but that I had to talk to the captain of the aircraft. Thus, I made it inside the plane, and introduced myself to the captain. With great politeness I regretted his predicament and told him that I had to be in Rawalpindi the next day where I was needed urgently to operate a nuclear reactor. The bluff worked, the captain was impressed, and I was allowed to stay on the plane.

The next hour, confusion reigned. The captain won an argument with the military and obtained fuel. The crew debated what to do, and most decided to return. A few more foreigners were allowed aboard later, as well as about 20 important-looking Pakistanis. Luggage and passengers were all in the cabin together. Near midnight the plane took off. It was the last plane for several days. The next few weeks saw hectic political activity with speeches, statements, strikes, and negotiations. Mujib was the de facto ruler of East Pakistan but did not have things sufficiently under control to prevent reported cases of atrocities against some West Pakistani citizens living in East Pakistan. Just when negotiations between President Yahya Khan and Sheik Mujibur Rahman seemed to be going well, the final crisis came. There was a tentative agreement, but it was unacceptable to West Pakistani leaders. Mujib remained firm, and the President, acceding to the objections, changed his mind, cut off negotiations, arrested Mujibur Rahman, declared him a traitor, and outlawed the Awami League. The country plunged into civil war. During the many political discussions at PINSTECH I had been determined to remain neutral. Soon, however, I found myself taking sides and disagreeing with most of my colleagues. Strangely enough, the other foreign visitors, consisting of the Polish engineers and a British professor assigned to the reactor school, had the same reaction.

My stay was coming to an end, and the experiment was ready to be performed. We needed at least 100 hours of reactor time. This represents only four days of around-the-clock operation, but at the rate of six hours per day for four to five days per week it would have required more than three weeks. Chances of equipment failure during such a long period are great. We started to agitate for continuous reactor operation. This was unheard of. There were only two competent engineers who could be in charge of shift operations. Other support departments also had inadequate manpower to cope with the problem. The reactor engineers were reluctant to set a precedent by working 12-hour shifts since their request for additional manpower had been turned down earlier, and they did not want continuous operation to become a habit. The laboratory director was not inclined to lose sleep over the problem. He told the engineers to do it if they could and to forget it if they couldn't.

Luckily the engineers (splendid fellows) succumbed to our persuasion and pleading and agreed to run the reactor. We all hoped that nothing would go wrong and nothing much did. On the last day the reactor scrammed as the result of a power failure. A trip to the power substation revealed employees happily performing routine maintenance. They assured us that they had informed PINSTECH as to their intentions but obliged us by turning the power back on. Our experiment was a success, and we collected the data we needed. The results are not analyzed yet, however, since PINSTECH will first have to negotiate with a Rawalpindi bank to obtain permission to use their computer. We felt a sense of accomplishment. More data collection, and work on other targets will now follow.

On one of my last days at PINSTECH I could not resist being ostentatious, and hoped I would not, as a result, be considered an Ugly American. I knew that laboratory parties were very popular. These were usually held in midafternoon. Tea and very sweet items called sweetmeats were served, together with oranges and other fruit. I decided to finance singlehandedly such a party for all shift workers involved with the memorable reactor operation. About 40 people showed up and devoured the sweetmeats with great gusto. In a speech, mandatory on such festive occasions, I pointed out that since all were worried about setting the precedent of continuous reactor operation, I was going to set another precedent. Anyone requiring continuous reactor operation must throw a party at the end. This will keep the requests serious. The cost of my extravagance? A total of $3.50. But then, that is more than a third of the janitor's monthly salary! A few days later, my work completed, I left. And to Pakistan, may the peace of Allah be with you.

Appendix II
Brief History of Pakistan's Nuclear Bomb Program[9]

At the time of my assignment in Pakistan, the official position was that its nuclear program was only pursuing peaceful applications of atomic energy. However, there were already signs that its leadership had other intentions. After the 1965 Indo-Pakistani War, which ended in a victory for India, the Minister of Foreign Affairs, Zulfikar Ali Bhutto, proclaimed: "If India builds the bomb, we will eat grass or leaves, even go hungry, but we will get one of our own."[10] Late in 1971, after I left PINSTECH, war once again broke out between India and Pakistan. Pakistan sustained heavy losses, and within two weeks it surrendered. This humiliation appeared to be a turning point in Pakistan's decision to build an atomic bomb. In 1972, Zulfikar Ali Bhutto, soon to be elected Prime Minister, instructed Pakistani scientists to build the bomb. Around the same time, Canada provided Pakistan with a 137-megawatt heavy

---
9 The views shared in this passage represent my personal perspective on the topic, which developed through observation, information, and reflection.
10 Singh, Khushwant, "Pakistan, India and The Bomb." *The New York Times*: July 1, 1979, Section E, Page 21.

water nuclear reactor that was installed at the Karachi Nuclear Power Plant and was soon producing weapons-grade plutonium.

In December 1974, however, the course of the Pakistani bomb program changed drastically with the return of German-trained metallurgist Abdul Quadeer Khan. He had spent the previous four years working for a nuclear fuel company on uranium enrichment plants and brought his vast knowledge of gas centrifuges to Pakistan. A. Q. Khan played a vital role in the success of Pakistan's nuclear program. He was placed in charge of a uranium enrichment plant which offered Pakistan a second and much simpler path to a bomb than the complicated plutonium route explained earlier. Although the uranium project began under Prime Minister Zulfikar Ali Bhutto, his influence over the project was short-lived. In 1977, General Muhammad Zia ul-Haq took power in a coup d'état and later hanged Bhutto in 1979. The military took control of the nuclear program, and it remains under their control today. On May 26, 1990, China tested a Pakistani bomb on Pakistan's behalf at one of its test sites. Finally, on May 28, 1998, less than three weeks after India's nuclear test, Pakistan exploded its first device at the Ras Koh test site in Baluchistan, starting a nuclear arms race between Pakistan and India which continues to this day.

Appendix III
A Note Regarding Scientific Publications

Over the time of my long scientific career, I have been a co-author of over 500 scientific articles, in refereed journals, conference proceedings, etc. Reference to some of the articles is made in the text of this Memoir. Unfortunately, I do not have a final and accurate count of all the articles I have co-authored, because several were published after my retirement, based on contributions I made to various experiments while still active. I have not kept track of these.

For me, one of the best measures of scientific output by any individual scientist rests with their published articles in refereed journals, in which they are listed as the first author, indicating their primary motivator and/or executor of the work. Of course, some articles are published in strict alphabetical order, as is the case in very large collaborations (WA80, WA98, PHENIX) or at the insistence of some of the authors, as was the case in the main paper associated with the story described in the "Orsay" vignette. (Gauvin,H, and D. Guerreau, Y. LeBeyec, M.

Lefort, F. Plasil and X. Tarrago, "Evaporation Residue Cross Sections from Reactions with Argon Ions. (*Physics Letters:* 58B, No 2, September 1, 1975.) Nevertheless, I present in this Appendix my first-author publications in refereed journals.

I published 10 articles as first author in refereed journals: 7 articles in the Physical Review (years 1965-83) and 3 articles in the prestigious Physical Review Letters (1978-84). I was the sole author on two of the PRL articles.

I was also the first author of an article written together with H. W. Schmitt entitled "Nuclear Fission" published in the Second Edition of the Encyclopedia of Physics, VCH Publishers, New York, (1991) p.817.

CPSIA information can be obtained
at www.ICGtesting.com
Printed in the USA
LVHW091253130321
681409LV00001B/4